THE GRANGE, WIMBLEDON

A Centenary Portrait

Beatrice Norman-Smith

THE GRANGE, WIMBLEDON
A Centenary Portrait

died Aug 1988

Douglas and Beatrice Norman-Smith

K.A.F. BREWIN BOOKS

Published by K.A.F. Brewin Books
Studley, Warwickshire.

First published 1984

Typeset in Press Roman
and printed in England by
Supaprint (Redditch)Ltd.
Redditch. Worcestershire.

ISBN 0 9505570 8 0

Contents

Plates

Preface

We have been involved for half of each of our lifetime, almost to the point of romantic attachment, in the place that forms the setting for this study. Without such involvement we should not have ventured on it; and we do not think we could have reached so deep into it.

In a real sense we feel we have been privileged to share and inherit something of the quintessence of time and place of this spot. Thus engaged, we have nevertheless done our level best to stand aside enough to see it for no more, *though also no less*, than it is, in terms of urban history.

Unlike Lewis Carroll's imperious characters, we cannot command our Alice, our browser, who picks up this book and dips into the middle:- 'Begin at the beginning, go on to the end, and then *stop*'. Instead, we have to put up warning signs, like, if you miss what we say here, you may find yourself thoroughly confused. One hundred years ago, there was a house on Wimbledon Common Southside that was called 'The Grange', at the time it was demolished in (probably) 1887. A road was cut through the gardens and grounds, south as far as the Ridgway, in 1888. The architect-surveyor, Richard Roberts, who drew the plans for the development of the road, and the surveyor to the Local Board called this new road 'Grange Road'; and so it seems to have been known when the first houses were built along the road in 1889. But already by 1890, and forever since, the road itself has been called 'The Grange', and not 'Grange Road'. In this book, we have tried to follow that historical sequence. Thus in Chapter 1, we refer to 'The Grange' throughout as meaning the original, basically eighteenth century *house*, on Southside. In Chapter 3, we describe how The Grange Estate was developed into Grange Road, from the months prior to the demolition of 'The Grange' house to the appearance of houses along 'Grange Road'; the houses being as specified in Chapter 5. From Chapter 5 onwards, we refer to 'The Grange' as *the road*, as did the Wimbledon Local Board, the occupiers of houses in the road, all directories, and electoral rolls, and, as it soon became known by custom and word of mouth.

This is the point where we can best acknowledge our several debts incurred in the making of this study. First to The Grange Preservation Association, who encouraged us over the three years it took us. To the Wimbledon Society (formerly John Evelyn Society) and especially its Local History Section, particularly its successive chairmen, Guy Parsloe and Richard Milward. To John Alman, who put his long experience at our disposal, and also read the proofs. To Wimbledon Public Library, especially its Reference librarians. To the Wimbledon Literary and Scientific Society. To the Public Record Office and the Surrey County Records Library. To Minet Archives Library of London history, under the auspices of Lambeth Borough Council; and to the Greater London Council in its several sections — the Historic Buildings section of the Architects' Department, and the History Library, photographic library, prints room and records department. To Guildhall Library, and that of the R.I.B.A. To the University of London Library. To the Royal Institute of Chartered Surveyors. To Hampton & Sons. To our several sources of oral evidence, virtually all of whom are acknowledged at the point in the text where we have taken their evidence into account. We should particularly refer to Miss Margaret Roney, who died on 4th October, 1983, just as we were starting to revise the text, and to Joe Burrell, who died six months before. We are grateful to them all, to A.P. Whitehead, and to the many others who have helped us in various ways, and who are, we fear, too numerous to mention. The list of sponsors, to whom we owe a special debt, is on page x. Help from Government Departments is seldom acknowledged. May we prove the exception by thanking in particular the Registrar-General and the Office of Population and Surveys for their help with censuses and registers of births, marriages and deaths, and wills. We also wish to thank all those who answered our many inquiries in the British Library Reading Room. Finally, it will be understood that we are neither of us architects. We recognised that the London Borough of Merton's Planning Department was housing historical treasure when we inspected there the original architects' drawings for houses erected in the road from 1889 on. These, especially those complete with their cellar and above-ground floor-by-floor elevations, enabled us to understand more than any other single source, the domestic economy of middle class society and housing 90 to 100 years ago.

Acknowledgements

The publisher wishes to acknowledge permission to reproduce the illustrations as follows: —

Mrs Alice Fowler	Plate 21
Greater London Council	Plates 8, 9, 12, 13, 16, 22
Guildhall Library	Plate 5
London Borough of Merton	Front cover and Plates 6, 10, 11, 14, 17, 18, 19, 20
Ordnance Survey	Plate 1
Wimbledon Society	Plates 2, 3 and 7

List of Sponsors

E.W. Bartley
Sir Cyril Black, J.P., D.L., F.R.I.C.S., The Sydney Black Charitable Trust
Rita Colman, Hon. Secretary, The Wimbledon Society
The Grange Preservation Association
London Borough of Merton
Richard Milward, M.A., Chairman, Local History Section, The Wimbledon Society
Norman Plastow, F.R.I.B.A.
Robin Reeve, Headmaster, King's College School, Wimbledon Common
Mrs. Rosemary Smith, Headmistress, Wimbledon High School (G.P.D.S.T.)
Robert Way, William Way (Wimbledon)Ltd.
Michael Young, (Lord Young of Dartington), Institute of Community Studies

1 'The Grange', The Original House & Its Occupiers (1747 - 1887)

The site and form of the original eighteenth century house can be seen with crossed hatching, as are also the coach house, cottages and out-buildings, on the 1865 Ordnance Survey map on Southside, Wimbledon Common [Plate 1]. At that time, it had no name, as was normal except for very large mansions. Houses were generally identified by the name of the current occupier. Hence the engravings are entitled 'Sir Francis Burdetts' [Plates 2 and 3]. The house was not named 'The Grange' until the late 1860s. In some literature it was called Wimbledon Villa and occasionally Wimbledon Lodge. This has caused lasting confusion and inaccuracy, as Wimbledon Lodge sometimes called Wimbledon Villa was the mansion on the Murray Road site adjacent. So for the sake of clarity we shall call the house 'The Grange' throughout its existence.

'The Grange' was built in 1747 by *Thomas Lewis* who lived there until his death in 1761. It continued in the occupation of his widow Mrs Mary Lewis until she died in 1762 and their spinster daughter Mary, the heiress, probably until she moved to Hawkhurst, Kent, about ten years before her demise in July 1796. All three were buried in St. Mary's Churchyard Wimbledon. The house that Thomas Lewis built is described as a 'three-storied edifice, of five bays, the central bay containing the door sheltered by two Ionic columns, supporting a pelmet, and a window above on each floor. This bay projected from the facade and was flanked by two windows on each storey on both sides of it. The roof supported a large weather vane. The house was approached by two pairs of iron gates. . .' [1]

The land attached to the property comprised a garden, pleasure grounds and meadow going down from Southside, Wimbledon Common, to the Ridgway [Plate 1]. The whole area was virtually identical to that covered by the present road, houses and gardens.

The 1787 James Corris map of the area marks 'The Grange' as *Hopkins*, and it is fair to assume that this was *Benjamin Bond Hopkins* (1744 – 1794). Hopkins was the heir of John 'Vulture' Hopkins, the successful South Sea Bubble speculator. Benjamin's heiress daughter Carloline married into the family of Mansel Baronetcy of County Carmarthen. Her husband Richard (1768–1844) had assumed his mother's maiden name of Phillips. Their elder son Courtenay (1801–1875) resumed the name and arms of Mansel. One of *his* sons was Richard Mansel Mansel (1850–1892). The unpublished MSS, 'The Mansel Family', B. Norman-Smith, deals in full with this complicated history of a family, many of whom from John 'Vulture' Hopkins onwards are buried in Wimbledon Parish Church. Benjamin was living at the eighteenth century Wimbledon House at the time, and was responsible for the construction of its lake and famous grotto built by *Bushell*, purchased the house and land when it came on the market on the removal of Miss Lewis in 1786. This was a common practice

1

(i.e. on removals or deaths) both of himself and his daughter *Caroline Phillips* (1774– 1850). They came to own a great deal of land and many houses in North Wimbledon especially around Wimbledon Common, and in South Wimbledon in the Cowdrey, Hartfield and Worple Road areas. Certainly *she* was the freeholder of 'The Grange' estate as were in turn her descendants until the whole property was sold by one of her grandsons, Richard Mansel Mansel in 1888. Consequently (except for a period when Caroline Phillips herself lived in it, and later, briefly, Richard Mansel Mansel) none of the occupants (list at Annex) were the freeholders but occupiers under unfurnished leases, some sufficiently long term for the people of Wimbledon to assume they they were the actual owners.

The principal early residents of 'The Grange' were *Henry, 2nd Duke of Newcastle* (and 9th Earl of Lincoln) (1720 – 1794) who was described by Horace Walpole "as dark and amorous and travestied by him in his 'Patapan or the Little White Dog.' He gave himself up to sport." He was the High Steward of Westminster from 1759 to his death which occurred at Palace Yard, Westminster on 22nd February 1794.

Next came the *Countess of Bristol* [2]. Was she Elizabeth, who married Frederick Augustus Hervey (1730–1803), 4th Earl of Bristol, in 1752, and who died 'suddenly of spasms' on 15th December, 1800, at Ickworth, Suffolk, seat of the Bristol family? Elizabeth's husband died of gout in Rome in 1803. 'He made sudden descents upon politics (Whig) and religion, not a figure to be taken seriously in either Church or Court, though he had the merits of a gadfly' [3]. This husband and wife appear to have lived apart. He was described as being a bad father and a worse husband.

The next and probably most famous of the residents was *Sir Francis Burdett* (1770– 1844) whose country house was 'The Grange' from about 1801 to at least 1812, with his wife Sophia, the very wealthy daughter of Thomas Coutts, the banker, and some of his children. The youngest daughter inherited the Coutts fortune. She, the Baroness Angela Burdett-Coutts (1814–1906) was a philanthropist and the friend of many famous men of art, literature and science. One of these was Charles Dickens who helped her in her role as Principal of Whitelands Training Institution for School-mistresses (now Whitelands College, West Hill, Putney).

To return to her father, Sir Francis (who succeeded his grandfather as baronet in 1797) and accounts of whose life and work can be read elsewhere; suffice it to say that he was an aristocratic Radical democratic politician, one of the champions of freedom of speech and of the individual. His chief claim to fame in Wimbledon, apart from his association with other political residents, such as John Horne Tooke, was his duel with *James Paull* [4], another Radical, who had been Burdett's friend. Circumstances surrounding their candidatures for a by-election for the City of Westminster parliamentary constituency, gave rise to a misunderstanding in May, 1807, as a result of which a duel between the two men took place in Coombe Wood, then on Wimbledon Common (now beyond the Kingston By-pass, the A3). Both were wounded in the leg, but a skilled surgeon allegedly "not being available in Wimbledon to visit him at 'The Grange' " , they went in the same carriage to London, where

2

Burdett was presumably seen at 80, Piccadilly, his town residence, by a metropolitan doctor. It was also from there, and not from his Wimbledon home, as some authors have stated, that he was arrested and taken to the Tower in 1810. The warrant had been issued by the Speaker of the House of Commons, who had voted an action of Burdett's a breach of privilege.

Arthur Eden (born 1793) was the son of Marianna and Thomas Eden, Virginia merchant with aristocratic origins, who lived at 'The Priory', Southside. Arthur lived in 'The Grange' from 1826–1833 and later went to live on Westside, Wimbledon Common. By 1851 he was an Assistant Controller, H.M. Exchequer.

Caroline Phillips (1774–1850) herself was at 'The Grange' in the 1830s and early 1840s, together with her son *Courtenay* at least in 1841.

From about 1843 – 1859 *the Reverend Richard Leonard Adams*, M.A., lived at 'The Grange'. He was the incumbent at the Wimbledon Parish Church having been licensed by the Bishop of London on 22nd May, 1846, and resigning the living to go to Shere in July, 1859. He contributed no doubt to the life of his church-goers and to the parish in general; for example he was chairman of the committee to set up the Wimbledon Village Reading Room, attached to the Village Hall, Lingfield Road. During his time in Wimbledon, he should have enjoyed not only 'The Grange', with its gardens and pleasure grounds but also Wimbledon Common, described in the 1840s as follows:-

"Wimbledon Common' – an elevated breezy and extensive waste, has long been noted for the delightful villas, hanging upon its outskirts. Its healthy situation, dry, *gravelly subsoil*, open unobstructed views, together with its pleasant proximity to London, have concurred to render property exceedingly valuable in this neighbourhood; the number of persons of rank, fortune and distinction, who have occupied from time to time the villas here, would make a catalogue of no ordinary longitude". [5]

The Reverend Adams had only a small personal income. He had no pew rents, about £100 in fees and Easter offerings, and £40 from Earl Spencer, the Lord of the Manor of Wimbledon. 'On Great Tithes, Glebe etc. was in the hands of Earl Spencer as Lay Impropriator, holding lives from the Dean and Chapter of Worcester. The supposed value was between £700 and £800 a year from which he pays £40 to the Perpetual Curate' (i.e. Reverend Adams in 1851). [6] It may seem strange that Adams was able to afford to pay the rent (unknown) to the Phillips/Mansel family, and about £7 per annum back to Lord Spencer under the Commutation of Tithes (1848) and support his family in such a large house as 'The Grange'. It is therefore assumed that substantial income came from his wife, born in 1807, as *Elizabeth Atherton Lilford*, a daughter of the 2nd Baron Lilford of Lilford Hall, with estates in Northamptonshire, Shropshire and Montgomery, and whose mother was the co-heir of Robert Atherton of Atherton Hall, Lancashire [7].

The Adams family appeared to live in the manner in which Elizabeth was presumably accustomed. The 1851 Census shows the couple with two sons and one daughter. The rest of the household comprised a lady's maid, a butler, a page, a nurse, and also

3

a cook, housemaid, and kitchenmaid.

There followed *Richard Garth* (1820–1903) who spent about six years (1860–66) in the house. He had been born Richard *Lowndes*, eldest son of the Reverend Richard Lowndes and Mary Douglas. His paternal grandfather William Lowndes had married Elizabeth Garth, the heiress to the Manor of Morden estates. The Lowndes assumed the name of Garth in 1837 when 'our' Richard was seventeen. In due course he became Lord of the Manor of Morden in 1862, whilst living at 'The Grange'. However he sold the Morden Park 185 acre estate only ten years later in 1872. He was not interested in being a landlord. The law was his chief love. Having been educated at Eton and Oxford, with a cricket blue, he started on his legal career, and was called to the Bar in 1847, taking silk in 1866. In the same year he became Conservative M.P. for Guildford until the next election in 1868, when he was defeated. He was apparently an able judge. In 1875 he was appointed Chief Justice of Bengal in Calcutta and was knighted in the same year. He remained in India for some ten years, then retired on ill health grounds, but he was sixty-five by this time anyway. Nevertheless he continued in England to take an interest in Indian affairs. He was buried in Morden in March 1903. His period of residence at 'The Grange' with his wife Clara and several children was the time of his increasing repute in the legal profession.

The first mention of the property under the name of 'The Grange' came with the advent of the *Elphinstone* family, who lived there from about 1867 to 1879.

Howard Warburton Elphinstone, J.P. (1830–1917) succeeded to the baronetcy in 1893, and was another barrister. He played some part in local affairs, being the vice-president of the Wimbledon Athenaeum, founded in 1877, (with Sir Henry Peek as President); and Merton Liberal Association (from 1880).

A letter headed 'The Grange' dated August 20th 1877 written by his wife, Mrs Constance Elphinstone, and addressed to Mrs. Peck, is reproduced as [Plates 4 and 4A]. By the time of Queen Victoria's jubilees *Lucy Peck* had acquired considerable repute in Britian and West Europe as a leading maker of wax dolls, with premises in Regent Street. Her work had unusual charm. [8] It seems likely that before her marriage she had been the governess to the Elphinstone children. [9] There were at least eight, the third to eighth being baptised at Wimbledon Parish Church from 1869 to 1879, and therefore born at 'The Grange'. The girls were born in 1869 and 1875.

The last tenant (from 1880) before the demolition of the house was *Captain Thomas Maude Roxby* (born 1830), who had retired from the 55th Regiment before coming to live in Wimbledon. Often heads of household seem to have been absent at Census date times. However, the Roxbys were at home at the time of the 1881 Census. The size of the household is therefore known. There were his wife, a daughter, two sons, his father-in-law and a visitor, and in addition originating in various other parts of the British Isles, a gardener, his wife and three children (presumably living in a gardener's cottage) and three unmarried female domestic servants.

According to his own evidence in his bankruptcy proceeding *Richard Mansel Mansel*

(1850–1892) also lived in the house (his own property) briefly prior to 1883; and probably on occasion thereafter until its demolition.

It is not known exactly when the house was pulled down, but probably about 1886/7. The bricks of the old building were advertised for sale in March 1888 [10]. This destruction was a deliberate act, preparatory to the creation of a road, originally called Grange Road, down the centre of the Estate (see Plate 1 again) with plots of land for sale by auction on either side. The story of this auction and the development of the Estate is described in Chapters 3 to 5.

'The Grange', in its 140 years, provided a home for a range of 'polite' society: noble, political, clerical, military, and professional.

If it is asked what part these relatively short-term leasehold occupants of 'The Grange' played in the general community life of Wimbledon village in educational, charitable, and cultural terms, the answer must be very little, with the exception of Reverend Adams, on account of his involvement as Rector of the Wimbledon Parish Church. Most if not all of them owned or rented London 'town' houses and/or other property in the British Isles and spent some of their time out of Wimbledon, apparently on at least some such occasions leaving their younger children at 'The Grange' in the care of governesses, nursemaids and servants.

There may, however, have been some social and intellectual intercourse between 'The Grange' and other big houses along Southside, Westside and Parkside all bordering Wimbledon Common. The houses either side which for clarity, we shall call Lingfield House and Murray House, were at the Common end of the roads so called today. The history of *Lingfield House* followed much the same pattern as 'The Grange'. It was another of Benjamin Bond Hopkins' purchases, bought by him in 1787 after the death of Ann, the widow of the original builders and owner, *Benjamin Hays*. Thereafter it was leased to various titled or political people, except for short periods when the freeholders (Bond Hopkins/Phillips/Mansel family) resided there.

Murray House (Wimbledon Lodge) however was built no doubt under a building lease, on land also owned by Benjamin Bond Hopkins, by *Gerard de Visme* in 1797 for his daughter. She married the *Hon. Sir Henry Murray*, who became a distinguished General. During her minority, there were also 'tenants' living in the house, notably Lord Bathurst and the Rt. Hon. Ladies Ashburnham, but from 1824 the Murray family occupied it until the death of the General's daughter *Miss Gertrude Murray* in 1904. The demolition of the house followed immediately and the sale of the Murray Estate to The British Land Company in 1905. The Murrays had acquired the freehold from *Edward Berkeley Mansel* (Richard's brother) only as recently as 1891.

Apart from such contact as they may have had with these neighbouring houses, the successive occupants of 'The Grange' undoubtedly 'knew', according to their particular interests, other military, national political, noble, merchant, families in the vicinity.

The manner in which this community changed as a consequence of the break-up of 'The Grange' Estate (and indeed of the Lingfield and Murray Estates) is now to be related.

Chapter 1 – Footnotes

[1] *'Old Wimbledon'*, Alfred Arber Cooke, Simpkin & Marshall, 1928.

[2] D.N.B. (see Bibliography)

[3] *'The British Establishment, 1760–1784'*, Alan Valentine.

[4] *'The Tragedy of a Comic Duel'*, Arthur Hawkes, Wimbledon & Merton Annual, Simpkins & Marshall, 1905, p.40.

[5] *'Environs of London'*, John Fisher Murray, William Blackburn, 1842, p.202.

[6] *'Ecclesiastical Census, 1851'*, P.R.O., H.O./129/47.

[7] Burke's Peerage & Baronetcy.

[8] *'History of English Dolls & Toys'* (Pollock's History), Kenneth & Marguerite Fawdry, 1979, p. 53.

[9] Lucy Peck was the mother of Lucy Norman whose birth is mentioned in the letter, and who in her turn lived with her husband Frank in the house in 'The Grange' (road), where the co-authors now live.

[10] *The Builder*, March, 1888 & the *Mid-Surrey Independent*, No. 598, 24th March, 1888.

6

The Original House on Southside, Wimbledon
(in its last years called *'The Grange'*)
built 1747   demolished 1887

Owners/Occupiers

1747–1761	Thomas LEWIS and family [1]	(buried 2.6.1761 in Wimbledon)	Owner/occupier
1761–1762	Mrs. Mary LEWIS – widow	(buried 26.1.1762 in Wimbledon)	Owner/occupier
1762–1786	Miss Mary LEWIS – daughter [2]	(buried 12.7.1796 in Wimbledon)	Owner/occupier

1787   Corris map marks house as Hopkins – presume
Benjamin BOND HOPKINS, who was living at Wimbledon
House at the time.   He probably bought the house
and land in 1786.   The freehold remained
in the family until the house was demolished
in 1887, and the land sold in 1888.
Consequently all the following (except Caroline
Phillips and Richard Mansel Mansel were not freehold owners but occupiers under leases.

1787–	Madame Allanson	Occupier
1791–1794	Duke of NEWCASTLE (2nd) [1,2] (died 22.2.1794)	Occupier
1795	Executors of Duke of Newcastle	
1796–1800	Countess of BRISTOL (Elizabeth, wife of Frederick, 4th. Earl. She died 15.12.1800) [1,2]	Occupier
1801–1812 at least	Sir Francis BURDETT [2]	Occupier
1822–1825	George BROWN Esq. [2]	Occupier
1826–c1833	Arthur EDEN Esq. [2]	Occupier
1835–1841	Mrs. Caroline PHILLIPS [2,3]	Owner/occupier
c1843–1859	Reverend Richard Leonard ADAMS [4]	Occupier
c1861 1866	Richard GARTH M.P. [5]	Tenant of Courtenay Mansel
1867/68– 1878/79	Howard Warburton ELPHINSTONE [2, 6]	Ditto until Courtenay Mansel died in 1875

7

1880–1882	Captain Thomas Maud ROXBY [7]	Tenant of Mansel Executors
c1882–1885	Sir Richard Mansel Mansel [8]	Owner/occupier
circa 1887	House demolished	

[1] 'Old Wimbledon' A. Arber Cooke: no other information

[2] Rate books – S.R.O. (There are a number of rate books missing – hence imprecision)

[3] 1841 Census

[4] Tithe map 1848 (and Wimbledon and Merton Annual 1910) and Rate books

[5] 1861 Census and 1865 Bartlett and Rate books

[6] P.O. Directories 1869–78 and 1871 Census – House first named 'The Grange'

[7] Kelly's Directory 1882 and 1881 Census

[8] Bankruptcy proceedings – Richard Mansel Mansel 1883

2 Wimbledon in the Last Third of Victoria's Reign

This period can be thought of as beginning with the enactment of the Wimbledon and Putney Commons Act of 1871.   Non-enclosure but conservation in perpetuity for public amenity had just begun to happen elsewhere around the London conurbation. Wimbledon was well in the forefront.   It contributed substantially to increasing the desirability of north Wimbledon for middle class villa residential development. Reference has already been made, in Chapter 1, to north Wimbledon being on a gravel elevation.   In the same year as the Act, Louis Napoleon's France was beaten by Prussia.   After the camp of 1888 the rifle volunteer movement National Rifle Association (N.R.A.) was removed to Bisley.   The N.R.A. grew out of fear of Louis Napoleon's Empire.   It had held an annual camp on Wimbledon Common, utilising much of the area between the Windmill and Southside.   In a growing residential suburb it came to be seen as a picturesque sideshow and as less important in its contribution to national defence.

By 1840, there was already a main line railway service through Wimbledon from Nine Elms (later from Waterloo, and later still, with a change at Clapham Junction, from Victoria).   But for another thirty years, there was little building development either in North Wimbledon or 'New' Wimbledon, south of the railway line.   In both, after 1871, development came fast; and in the 1890s, after the District Line was extended from Putney Bridge to Wimbledon, Wimbledon Park was also developed, quickly.

Despite the railways, it was still an age of *real* horse-power, not just of horse-power as a measure of energy.   The residences of that time were built mainly for people who used their legs for walking;   and for a minority who rode, or had a carriage and horse(s) to drive.

In 1861, when Earl Spencer as Lord of Wimbledon Manor, put forward his proposals for enclosure of the Commons, he cannot have been alone in thinking of Wimbledon as perhaps an expanding village.   With 4,644 population, few can have thought of it as a town, even potentially.   Yet in the next decade, its population had doubled; and in the next thirty years its growth rate was as high as almost anywhere in the conurbation and the country as a whole.

Victorian challenge and response.
The 'Wimbledon at the accession of Queen Victoria' which John Townsend saw as a young man (and recollected in the *Wimbledon & Merton Annual, 1903)* was utterly feudal.   The Reverend William Bartlett's standard *History* was written, and published in 1865, just as the comparatively long and slow preceding epoch came to a close. Bartlett reflects an atmosphere of there being time for everything and of everything being in its place.

The decades that followed saw *that* Wimbledon challenged from without and within; and responding positively, radically, and yet conservatively.   It is no part of the responsibility of this study to examine all the aspects of the response.   But the microcosm we shall be examining needs to be prefaced, particularly for non-Wimbledon readers, by some sign-posting of major features of the response and heralding the years that followed on the decades of urgency up to the outbreak of the first World War.   Signposting is perforce selective; and we have no space to spare for academic justification for our selection.

First, as we indicated at the start of this chapter, we would put the establishment of the largely elected board of Wimbledon and Putney *Commons Conservators*, following the statute of 1871, charged with the duty 'to keep the Commons open and un-enclosed, protecting the turf, gorse, trees and other natural products and preventing wanton destruction of birds'.   This was the first *novelty* in (local) government.

Second, and third, were two pre-existing pieces of local government.   Developed, to some extent re-staffed if not re-modelled, they played an even more important part in the response-processes than any of the novelties.

The second, was the local government machine as this is more narrowly defined. There had, for some decades, been a *Wimbledon Local Board*, as the main alternative to the vestry and the manorial court for purposes of regulation.   In historical perspective, until the late 1880s the W.L.B. had not been at all that effective.   During the late 1880s it first trained and then elected as chairman John Townsend (see chapter 4).   It had a small team of professional officers, notably Santo Crimp as its surveyor and Dr Pocklington as its Medical Officer of Health.   Townsend and his elected colleagues were few, mostly conservative in politics, and interested, sometimes in the sense of 'having to declare an interest' in the developments they were concerned with regulating.   They took their duty to be, if not actually promoting, at least not hindering, the remarkable town growth of Wimbledon required by the population increase.

The third was an institution as ancient as the vestry and manorial court, the *Magistrates' Bench*.   During the population explosion, it helped to keep order, and protect persons and property, and did it without fuss or, generally, getting reported in the press.

As regards *the press*, improvement in local newspaper coverage to the extent as justified in proportion to the extra potential readers, occurred only just before the outbreak of the first world war.   What *did* come much earlier, was the improvement of the *education and free library services*.   In education, 1871, the date we cited in the first reference at the start of this chapter, was also the parliamentary session in which the Forster Education Act became law.   This empowered school boards to set up schools in their districts.   The *parochial* boards in Wimbledon resisted, cajoling subscribers for more money from private sources to increase and expand parochial schools in lieu of public rate-supported schooling;   and for years, until after the first world war, succeeded in presenting theirs as a credible alternative.   There were resemblances of philosophical argument and counter-argument in the debates in the early 1880s about setting up a free public library. Again, at its start, private subscription in money and in books played some part in the Library. It was only after six years of open argument that the public library opened in 1887. In retrospect it may be seen as the essential step towards the creation of a thinking, albeit not yet fully enfranchised electorate. Progressively, it democratised, where Richardson Evans, through the John Evelyn Club from 1903 was creating a local elite of leaders of thought on amenity matters. Ever since these two events, both property-owning and non-property-owning Wimbledon has been subject to public scrutiny, opposition, interest and involvement.

3 The Grange Estate Auctions

With what must have been a good deal of pre-auction expenditure, Richard Mansel Mansel's Wimbledon estates were sold off, albeit at the second time of asking. Plots of land were sold in a small part directly to intending occupiers, but in the main to a few speculators, at *The Mart, Tokenhouse yard,* St. Bartholomews Lane, an appropriate City and national, becoming international set of auction rooms, in 1888. [Plate 5]   In the main, locals in the know bought in. We shall see [Chapter 4] that two at least had good political and business training prior to engaging in this enterprise.

The First Auction
This took place in February 1886, at no doubt an earlier date than the economic climate would have suggested prudent, but Richard Mansel Mansel's bankruptcy in 1883 demanded the premature essay.   An attempt was made to sell the whole 'Grange' Estate of some seven acres as one lot, but the bid of £8000 was not considered acceptable and the property was withdrawn.   It must then have been decided that more money might be raised if a road to be called Grange Road was built through the centre of the estate, and the land on either side sold as individual building lots.

The Roberts Valuation Report
To this end, Sir Richard and his Trustees had a valuation report prepared for this estate and also for the Wimbledon Hill estate (including what became Mansel, Raymond and Malcolm Roads) and the ground rents for the Wimbledon High School (the Girl's Public Day School Trust establishment sandwiched into a tiny site at the foot of Wimbledon Hill) and the Trinity Presbyterian Church built in 'Mansel Road' in 1885.   The report contained valuations of other Wimbledon ground rents including some in Lingfield Road and Ridgway Place.

The report made by Richard Roberts of 42 New Broad Street, E.C., architect and surveyor on 24th September 1886 states that the valuation of the estate in the Wimbledon document is part of a vaulation of properties, mostly in Swansea, Wales, some in Limpsfield, Surrey, prepared in connection with a loan for £25,000.

The Second Auction
In the event, neither The Grange Estate nor the Wimbledon Hill estate nor other Wimbledon Mansel property came up for auction again until July 2nd 1888.   This time, Walker & Runtz, chartered surveyors & auctioneers of Chigwell Street, at the top of Moorgate, north of the Bank of England, and east of the Temple, where John Ignatius Williams, solicitor, one of Richard Mansel's Trustees under his father Courtenay's will, had come out of Wales to operate, and the generally more optimistic confidence climate that prevailed as the Great Depression drew to its slow close, did

12

the trick.   The other Trustee was Charles Norton, a solicitor of Swansea who figures in the bankruptcy proceedings.

So Richard withdrew from the Wimbledon scene, leaving only restrictive covenants (albeit of considerable value to conservationists) plus a name for the Mansels to be remembered by as one passes the High School on the way through Raymond Road and the 'slips' to Sunnyside and the Ridgway, going uphill home to The Grange (road) from the station and a day's work in town.

The sale was very largely attended.   'The Grange' Estate, now described as 'ripe for immediate building operations' was offered in 48 lots.   It seems likely that the size as well as the number of lots offered corresponded very closely to Richard Roberts' plan (not reproduced) attached to his report of 24th September 1886.   This showed plots for 48 possible houses, (16 detached and 16 pairs of semi-detached), with roughly 50 feet frontages on to the road, with the exception of the corner houses on Southside which were to have longer frontages onto Grange Road.   The amounts raised from some of the plots are quoted in 'The Builder' as follows:- 3 plots at £400 each, 6 plots at £300 each and 20 at £250 each.   This total of £8000 only accounts for 29 lots, so the total proceeds for 'The Grange' estate must have greatly exceeded the amount of £8000 offered for the whole undivided estate at the first auction.

It is interesting to note that 'the entire proceeds of the day's work, including the ground rents amounted to upwards of £26,000.'   So the Wimbledon property alone raised more than enough to cover the £25,000 loan to Sir Richard without any proceeds from any sale of his Welsh properties.   We do not know if such a sale took place.

Had Roberts' housing plan been followed, the road to-day would have presented a very different appearance with many semi-detached houses and the detached houses all close together on very small plots of land.   In the event, only 23 dwellings were built where 48 had been proposed.   The 23 comprised 5 houses with stables and coach-houses attached, 16 other detached houses and only one pair of semi-detached.   The present 38 Ridgway/12 The Grange, described as a pair of houses, was built on the land which had been sold to the Wimbledon Local Board before the auction.   It follows that far from the non-corner houses having only 50 feet frontages, they ranged from 60 feet in the case of 4 houses, through the 70–90 feet band up to 137 feet (present No. 1) and 150 feet (No. 26 – now present No. 26 plus No. 25).

Purchasers at Second Auction
The reason for the great variety of frontage lengths was (and is) probably that only three people, Sir Henry Peek, John Townsend and Henry Harmer, whose lives and activities are described in Chapter 4, purchased most of the lots between them.   They were thus able to allocate frontages of their respective blocks of lots as circumstances required.   Although no list of the buyers of the lots at the auction sale of July 1888 has survived it has been possible to establish from various deeds, that Sir Henry Peek bought the lots on the north-east side of the road to about half way down to the Ridgway.   This was the land on which the present Nos. 1, 2, 3, 4, 5, 6 and 7, with its

coach-house, were built. (The three lots on the north-east Southside corner on which 'Grangemuir' and its coach-house were built were bought directly at the auction by Robert T. Thomson.) The finalisation date making Sir Henry the beneficial owner was the 6th December 1888, and he made haste in 1889 to sell off the lots, from one to four in number to a variety of 'applicants'. (Were they friends or acquaintances?) It is clear that several of the first house occupants were already local people who had been living in earlier North Wimbledon roads. A more detailed description of these sales follows later.

The remaining plots (including later that which had been sold by Sir Richard to the Wimbledon Local Board for £3000 before the 1888 auction) down the eastern side of the road to the Ridgway (present Nos. 8, 9, 10, 11, and 12 The Grange/38 Ridgway) were acquired by John Townsend. By 1891 he had built on this land one house (No. 8) on commission, and the remainder for leasing out on probably 21 years leases in the first instance. In other words he bought the lots of land at the auction, erected the buildings himself, in the main as a speculative builder, after negotiating his way through the building regulations of the Local Board of which he was chairman.

Going northwards from the Ridgway on the west side of the road, the corner plot with land fronting onto the Ridgway together with plots on Grange Road were probably bought at the auction by Sir Joseph Bazalgette, though we have no deeds to prove this. He certainly had the house, 'Grange Lodge' built on these lots. The remaining lots up as far as the present No. 26 and on which the present Nos. 15, 16, 17, 18, 19, the unbuilt on land (now part of 'Grange Close', 54 Murray Road), 22, 23, and 24, were built were purchased at the auction by Henry Harmer, the other builder. He had borrowed money to do so, mainly from John Churchill, a Wimbledon resident with offices at 11 New Burlington Street, London as a medical publisher! Harmer appears to have hoped to sell the freehold land outright either for others to build upon, or to be given the contract to build the house for the new freeholder. It took him some years to achieve this end, the houses being built only over a period of ten years. In the event he had to erect in 1897 and lease out one house (present No. 16).

The remaining lots on the west side of the road were bought by other people at the auction. The land on which the present No. 26 (plus No. 25) stands, by one John Cross; and the 3 lots on which 'Canisbay' and its coach-house were to be built (present No. 29, The Grange/3,Southside and No. 27, The Grange) by James Robert Malcolm.

The Building of the Houses
All houses erected were large villas. Why were such large houses built particularly in some instances with so little ground around them, in spite of more than one auction lot of 50 foot frontage being allocated to the various houses? The answer is probably twofold. First the *covenants* laid down at the auction (which still apply to-day) as to which see Appendix I. Second, the *boundaries*, and consequent *shape* of The Grange Estate.

The Boundaries
The Grange Estate [Plate 1 1865 Ordnance Survey Map] was not rectangular in shape,

14

and was bounded on the east by the Lingfield Road/Lingfield House Estate. This boundary was formed by a seven foot high brick wall erected presumably when the 18th century 'Lingfield House' was built at a date prior to 'The Grange' house. The wall ran and still runs from Southside, Wimbledon Common to the southern end of the present No. 7's back garden; and represented the length of Lingfield House's garden and pleasure grounds. The remaining acreage of the former Lingfield House estate, to the Ridgway, although belonging to the Lingfield House owners, was already built upon by the time the Grange Estate was auctioned in 1888. It had been pasture land with a sheep walk on the west side (continuing across the Ridgway), and an avenue of elm trees separating it from the Grange Estate.

This 'Sheep Walk' (the name by which it is known to-day) became a Private Road when the Lingfield Road houses (present Nos. 27–31 and the original No. 32 on which Lingfield Court now stands) were built in 1871/2.

In consequence the back gardens of the present Nos. 8–12 The Grange (road) are considerably shorter than No. 7's. It also accounts for the fact that their gardens are mainly at the side rather than the back of their houses.

On the west side the Estate was bounded by the Murray House ('Wimbledon Lodge') garden, pleasure grounds and meadows. The Murray Estate was not developed until 1905 (Chapter 8). Consequently the Grange Road houses on the north west side also originally had short back gardens. The original owner of No. 26 remedied this by buying additional auction lots at the *side* of the house. Several owners of these same north west houses (including No. 26) bought Murray Estate land in 1905 to extend their *back* gardens further westwards.

4 The Middlemen

Mention has already been made of the middlemen involved between the original selling landowner, Sir Richard Mansel Mansel, and the bulk of the original purchaser occupiers. In Chapter 5 we analyse each of the original houses, and where appropriate, append brief professional biographical material about the architects responsible for their design. In Chapter 6, we analyse the original occupiers by sex, marital and family condition and by social class/occupation. Before proceeding to those two, inevitably longer chapters, which because they were concerned so vitally with the determination of the character of the road, have been treated as the core of this study, we felt that we should set down in the present chapter something more about the three most important middlemen. The importance of the first for the road is more indirect than direct. His direct connexion lasted for less than a year. This was Sir Henry Peek, M.P. The other two were the two speculative builders, also local Wimbledon men, who bought significant chunks of lots at the second auction, and retained the freeholds for several years, John Townsend, and Henry Harmer. Both these men were not *just* speculative builders.

Peek and Townsend knew some local celebrity in their lifetime; and Townsend also on his death. Harmer, for his part, was left in unsung obscurity in life and at death; but we here assess his part, along with that of Peek and Townsend, in the making of Grange Road (now The Grange).

Sir Henry William Peek (1826–1898) M.P.
Peek was the top half of Frean, his father having been the biscuit Peek. Peek rose to the top *via* the Dorking and mid-Surrey parliamentary elections to the House of Commons in the Conservative interest. The family business enabled him and his lady-wife to ensconce themselves as doyens of Wimbledon House, its gardens and grounds in the mid-nineteenth century. Peek earned his way into local acceptance in the 1860s. He spearheaded the parliamentary and extra-parliamentary campaign of attrition to frustrate Lord Spencer's shot at getting *Wimbledon Common* enclosed. The Wimbledon & Putney Commons 1871 Act ten years after the latter started his manorial lord's ploy, finally saw Spencer off from Wimbledon.

Not only did the 1871 Act buy the Common, and in effect also, the manor, out of feudalism; by preserving its amenities, it made it suitable for desirable bourgeois development. There were three additional, relatively minor, rearrangements required to complete the job. Peek, now as a Commons Conservator as well as an M.P. had a hand 'in effecting all three. First was the suppression of such habits of the former commoners as gorse-burning. The second was the prevention of the proposal by the London and South Western Railway, to put a railway across the common. Peek fought this from December, 1880, with the full support of the Wimbledon bourgeois commuters who felt, early, that the best way to stop the impertinent replies, as they saw them, to their representations to the Railway Company for improved facilities was the tried Victorian remedy of competition. As 'Glenrosa' wrote in the *Surrey Independent* on 11th February, 1888, "When the District Line arrives (from Putney Bridge, an event perhaps even more eagerly awaited by Mr. Beaumont of Wimbledon Park House) with its third class carriages, the (L. & S.W.R.) Company will perforce have (to change its attitude)'. This happened within the next two years. It was smartly followed by speculative terrace semi-detached housing round Wimbledon Park District Line and Southfields stations, and by the lines of detached bourgeois houses with views over the — now — new golf course (largely) park, down Home Park Road and Arthur Road. Peek's third act of consolidation of bourgeois amenity also concerned the Common. This was to end the long association of the National Rifle Association with the Common, and its use of it for its annual camp and prize shoot. The *Independent* was already pointing out the cost of keeping up the tradition, in its issue of 19th, March 1881, noting the amount of damage it did annually for its £100 p.a. rent. It was not just the damage to the Common, and the risk to the bourgeois users from a stray bullet (or, now, a golf-ball); it was that the birth rate always increased nine months after each camp.

Peek and the people, professionals, bourgeois *haute*, like Miss Peache, and petit, he ushered in as late-Victorian replacements for manorial government, trotted briefly on stage instead, generally performing the various good works looked for from successors to manorial lords and their ladies. Amongst other things they served during its first 20 years on the management committee of the Wimbledon Village Club.

At the age of 68, and helping to establish a fashion that has been more democratic for the last two or three generations, Peek, with four years left of life, retired to Devon. His son then sold out for development. Hampton and Sons were the newly-come to Wimbledon estate-and managing-agents chosen for the operation. Their office, still as erected at the south-east end of Wimbledon Common Parkside and Marryat Road, at what had been the exact south-west corner of Peek's estate, remains as a redolent reminder of what became *the* Wimbledon Common housing development feature of the Edwardian age; which it has remained ever since. Parkside, Peek Crescent, Parkside Gardens, and Calonne Road, were the physical result of that development. So much for Peek's important *indirect* influence on suburban middle class development in North Wimbledon. As to his *direct* concern with 'Grange Road', from inspection of deeds of properties in The Grange, we found that, as already specified in Chapter 3, in his early sixties, Peek dabbled in speculation in land values when Mansel was selling off the Grange Estate plots, six years before Peek retired to Devon.

Peek's wife was otherwise engaged, in the mode approved by patriarchal society. She gilded the garden lily her husband had bought for a song after Lady Marryat, during her long widowhood, had beautified it. With his wife gone before, and his pickings collected from the area *he* had helped to beautify for perpetuity, together with his equities, and leaving his son to realise on the Wimbledon House estate, Peek also, but in a more substantial puff of improvement-profit than Mansel had managed to raise, vanished also, like a pantomime fairy, from the Wimbledon scene.

While they were in full flush at *Wimbledon House*, as recorded in the 1881 Census, the

Peeks lived in some style. Sir Henry William Peek was then 56 years old, a coffee and spice merchant; Lady Margaret, his wife, was 52. He was a baronet, and an M.P. Cuthbert, their son, aged 26, unmarried, B.A., Cambridge, student of law, lived in Wimbledon House with them. Edwin Caldecott, aged 52, Sir Henry's brother-in-law, was with them on census night, together with his wife and four unmarried children. Also in Wimbledon House itself were a cook, a lady's maid, three housemaids, a kitchenmaid, and a footman. And in Wimbledon House lodge and the gardeners' cottages in the grounds were six gardeners and three stockmen.

When it came to the more prosaic end recorded in his will, as published on probate (to Sir Cuthbert Edgar Peek, Baronet, in November, 1898), Sir Henry Peek left effects of £418,585.

So our Peek was able to leave, both Wimbledon, as he envisioned it, along with many of his middle class contemporaries, *and* his family, well-provided-for, at least in his terms, at his death at the age of 74. And, as we shall see, in the next two chapters, The Grange, as part of that legacy, was, by then, well on its way to accomplishing the *embourgeoisement* which he must have seen as its manifest destiny.

John Townsend (1823–1917) J.P.
Richard Mansel had managed to make his way as a newcomer, a *nouveau*, though never *riche*, into a mature baronetcy. Peek was a bourgeois, who collected a baronetcy, as well as land and further respect and material wealth. Townsend's father was a 'victualler'. John seems to have been a poorish country boy, who made it, by virtue of marriage, *via* a business in a village that was about to sprout into a town, and by public service and discreet private enterprise in which his knowledge acquired through public service came in useful, into the top rank of the petty bourgeoisie; and, finally, into what Wells called the 'squirearchy of the underling', the magisterial bench.

But in terms of urban development, Townsend, as compared with the more remembered Peek, should be seen as equally important, unduly neglected – quite apart from his not collecting any of the *national* honour he rated in his age and time. He 'had come to Wimbledon when still a very young man', from upbringing unrecorded except for Aston Brompton, Oxfordshire, born February 1823.

He married into a Wimbledon building firm, '*Parsons*', when it was in a small way, like Wimbledon itself; and elevated it and the town, in the unretired years of an active Victorian lifetime, prior to his death at the age of 94, all but, in January, 1917, in the borough he had made but of which he was not even ever made a freeman. If politics is unforgiving, then local government politics is a serpent's tooth. More probably than anyone else, as a master builder and for several years chairman of the Wimbledon Local Board until it was reorganised in 1894, with other bits of effective and less effective local government he shaped what became the Borough of Wimbledon, as much anyway as Peek shaped the post-Spencer Common. But Townsend's household, in the 1861 to 1881 Censuses, and his wealth, as measured by his effects on probate in 1917, may be assessed as one-twentieth those of Peek.

Townsend was no vulture. His was the role of sparrow, picking up the crumbs falling

18

from Mansel's and Peek's linen-laid tables; opportunist yet hardly noticeable save by 'Glenrosa', the acidulated columnist of the *Surrey Independent*, who never failed to take the chance of a snide comment on Townsend's public record, with animadversions on the unrewarded aspirations of 'poor "Sir John"'; 'Glenrosa' had led, or echoed, his, as far as we can trace the evidence, unvoiced hopes, into unmet expectations of a knighthood during the first royal jubilee honours of 1887.

'Nil mortuis'. It took from Townsend's retirement from politics, past sorrows at the death of his only two sons, and after he had spent his last twenty years in public service still as a J.P., for him to earn only with his own death, obituary recognition of his worth, from 'Glenrosa's' successor. For the text for his funeral oration, the rector of Emmanuel Church (next door to the corner of Lingfield Road, the Ridgway and the south-eastern end of The Grange) took the passage 'And David, after he had served his generation according to the will of God, fell to sleep'; and ended his address by begging 'God that all present might at the end be found to have served God and their generation so devotedly'.

Enough of the hard-won plaudits of the professional mourners of one's next generation. As a builder, Townsend was not simply a large pebble in a local pool. His getting large contracts to build in Gower Street, Bloomsbury and on the Marine Parade, Brighton, showed that he had more than a Wimbledon repute. The houses round the corner from his own residence (No. 14, Lingfield Road), however, are what most concern us; Townsend's role in respect of them has already been specified in Chapter 3. We shall have more to say of the subsequent history of these properties in The Grange.

There is one further incident, however, which illustrates the suspicion with which such a public figure with private and adjacent interest was treated by scrutineers of his activities, proposals and motives. In terms of land and possible profit from it, it was nothing. Had what he proposed been accepted, a mess that has gone on a further hundred years might have been avoided. But because he had to be above reproach he offered not to pursue it.

It was reported to the *Wimbledon Local Board* at the beginning of February, 1890, that Townsend was willing to give a slip of land between the shops next to Emmanuel Church and the corner of Grange Road, if the Board would make up a pathway, kerb and concrete it. One of Townsend's backers characterised it as a generous offer, adding that the cost of the works to the Board would be about £10.00, whereas the value of the land in question was £65, and the Ridgway was different from a private road. It would be a great boon to the inhabitants if they could walk up to The Grange (road) on a good pathway, and if the offer was not accepted they would have to purchase the land at some later date. Dr. Little opposed and Mr. Hamshaw considered it a dangerous precedent. Townsend said there seemed to be some misunderstanding and he would withdraw his offer. His original backer however pressed his motion to a vote, in which the issue was 6 to 4 in favour. As Chairman of the Board, Townsend's overall influence in the creation of the road ramified much more widely than the houses he built, he knew its overall potential rateable value, and could

19

assess the priority it merited in building regulations approvals, weekly watering of the road surface, and adoption and paving. It achieved such maturity relatively quickly.

Townsend was not alone in being pulled up short by the Board, which was glad enough to re-elect him to its chairmanship year after year until, with the Board's impending replacement by a larger Council in 1894, he retired, not seeking to reoffer himself for election to the new set-up.

Probate of his will in 1917 showed him leaving effects to the value of £35,000. He bequeathed, along with other items to his daughter, Frances Sophia Boag, the 'silver tea and coffee service presented to me in 1895 by the inhabitants of Wimbledon', and in 'trust to my wife, thereafter to Charles Melville Townsend, grandson, absolutely if he reaches the age of 21, the chiming clock presented to me by the inhabitants of Wimbledon'.

Townsend told a House of Commons Select Committee in March, 1883 that he was the owner of twenty houses in 'Upper Wimbledon'; and that an adequate supply of water was greatly needed.

He had been a leading member of the Wimbledon Division Conservative Association, but neither those who went along with his political party and its adherents among the Board's members, nor members representing wards in 'new' Wimbledon, south of the railway, were prepared to let him stray beyond precedent or into unsanctioned initiative. The Board found him *useful*. Proposing his re-election to the chair in April, 1887, Mr. Casswell said 'his being about Wimbledon all day really was an asset'.

'Sparrows can't sing'; but we have tried to string together the sum of Townsend's peckings and chirrupings. As soon as the seven acres of fields that made up the back-lands between the gardens of the old 'Grange' house and the Ridgway were put under their new crop of building land with each house its garden, during Townsend's last few years on the old Local Board, there descended, like so many starlings, a whole covey of architects, surveyors, auctioneers, estate agents, conveyancing solicitors, restricted only by their clients and the covenants set by Mansel, all ultimately reflecting their interpretation of maximum benefit within the prevailing market forces and compliance with the requirements of building regulations and conventions established as case law by the Local Board with the advice of its professional officers. The latter numbered only *four*; the Town Clerk, the Board's Treasurer, the Board's Surveyor, and its Medical Officer of Health.

Townsend stayed in business until he was seventy, in 1893; and in the chair of the Local Board until 1894. Thereafter he doubtless remained the elder statesman both in the firm of Parsons & Townsend; and became a responsible member of the Wimbledon Magistrates' bench, as a J.P. — and may well have been consulted on occasion after the Board was replaced by the successive newer forms of local govern-ment authority, on a diminishing number of matters. As a business, 'Parsons & Townsend' continued to take a two page spread advertisement space in the local directories for many years after John Townsend's 'retirement from business life when he had reached the age of 70'; indeed until 1913, operating as builders and decorators

20

and also as estate agents, auctioneers, valuers, funeral furnishers and monumental masons. Townsend had earned his obituaries in the Wimbledon Borough News and its editor's comment, together with the mark of respect shown by Sir Arthur Holland and the rest of the bench, and the tribute by the Rev. E.W. Moore of Emmanuel Church at his funeral service, wherein his interest in the aged poor of the almshouses was also remarked as very 'devoted'. He also rated a monumental memorial in the form of a headstone in the cemetery of St. Mary's, Wimbledon parish church, along with various of his descendants, his first wife's parents (Parsons – the foundation, along with his native powers, of his career and fortune), and his second wife and widow, Charlotte Hollier, who survived him. She died at the age of 79, on 28th March, 1920.

However major one's contribution to the public and common weal, that seems to be all one earns in public recognition of it, at the end; unless resuscitated by the casual notice of historians, as now.

Henry Harmer (1837–1926)
The third figure in this chapter is like the second to the extent that he too was a builder, living and working in the main – and to an even greater extent than Townsend in the latter respect – locally. The size of his business, as measured by the number of his employees, was also much the same as Townsend's:- 40-50 men, and 9 boys. Harmer never went into national politics, like Peek; nor local politics, like Townsend. And, again, unlike the other two, he never married. He was also more 'local' than the other, both older, two; albeit his origins are slightly more obscure even than Townsend's. But we reckon it as 90 per cent certain that he was the son of Charles and Mary Ann Harmer. Charles, according to the 1861 Census, was born in Wimbledon in 1813. In 1861, Charles was a carpenter, employing one man and a boy, and living at No. 11, Lingfield Road, together with his wife, and his son, Arthur, aged 20, also a carpenter. By the time of the 1871 Census, Charles, while still living at No. 11, was now a 'builder employing four men'. Their son Arthur had moved to No.10 next door, with, then, a wife and small daughter. He was still occupied as a carpenter, but had also by that date become the Clerk to the Wimbledon Parish Vestry, and the Sexton. By 1881, Charles was dead; his widow still lived at No. 11 in what was described as house 'and workshop'. Arthur and his family were still at No.10; but he was no longer described as a carpenter. Moreover the entry of Vestry Clerk was crossed through, in favour of 'Registrar of Births, Deaths and Marriages', which post Arthur held for some years thereafter. Ten years further on, according to the 1891 Poor Rate Book, No. 11 was in the owner-occupation of *Henry* Harmer, a builder, operating from an address in Worple Road, where he had also been living, and in which area he leased land from the Mansel family. Henry continued his work from Worple Road, had acquired a considerable interest in land in Grange Road, and had also bought the freeholds of Nos. 6 to 10, Lingfield Road. All the houses on that side of Lingfield Road had been built as leasehold properties. Their freeholds remained with the Mansel family until they were sold off by them in the 1870s and 1880s. According to the 1881 Census, Henry was aged 44, unmarried, born in Wimbledon, living with his unmarried sister, Martha, and their unmarried 17 years-old servant, Kate Ellis, born in Chertsey.

Henry Harmer's building work in Grange Road is recounted in Chapter 5. Of his practice, more generally, we have found no instance extending beyond Wimbledon; but he was certainly not confined to purely domestic building. In May, 1891, he submitted an accepted tender for £778.10s., for additions *and alterations to the Wimbledon Sanitary Laundry, Cranbrook Road, off Worple Road.* In those days, laundering was big business. No nylon, washing machines in the home, or laundrettes. Harmer, with premises in Worple Road, was appropriately in on the Cranbrook Road Laundry expansion.

Some of Harmer's employees resembled Tressall's *'Ragged trousered philanthropists';* [Appendix II] It may be salutary to fancy that such may have been the men and boys who built Nos. 5, 6, and 16, The Grange.

Henry Harmer had just reached his 'teens at the time of the 1851 Census; Wimbledon's population then was 2,693. At his death, in 1926, the year of the General Strike, when he had reached the age of 89, just five years short of Townsend's count in 1917, the population had reached as high as it has ever gone, about 59,000. Some obsolete houses have been knocked down since Harmer died; and some new units built. But the basic housing stock was built by Townsend and Harmer and their men and boys, and other small-scale local builders. They probably bought their supplies from the builders' merchant firm founded in 1867 by Thomas Way, the great grandfather of Robert, who is now the head of William Way (Wimbledon)Ltd.

Harmer made his will in 1925; and left effects of almost the same *money* value as Townsend had done; £39,569 (cf. Townsend, £35,000). Harmer bequeathed it to his various nephews, nieces, grand-nieces, and housekeeper, nine pieces of it in the form of properties in land/houses in Wimbledon; the rest of it in monies/their equivalents in 12 equal shares and 2 half shares; other than two specific sums, one of £200, bequeathed to Mrs. Lottie Tomlinson, his housekeeper. It would seem that the men whom Henry made his executors (one of whom, Walter Scott, J.P., of Kingston-upon-Thames, to whom he bequeathed £100, was probably not a relative, as presumably was also the case with Mrs. Tomlinson) had gone up in the world as compared with Henry. His nephew executor was a civil servant; his grandnephew executor, an engineer.

His death, in 1926, as we have noted, coincided with the General Strike; when the Wimbledon Borough News was congratulating itself, editorially, on still managing to give its readers 8 pages. Whether because of pressure on space on that account, or because none of his kin inserted a notice in its 'Deaths' inches; or, perhaps, if the W.B.N. reckoned Henry Harmer in 1926 too obscure a figure to merit it, no obituary of him ever appeared, as far as we have been able to trace. We trust this brief account of him may have gone a small part of the way needed to put the record straight.

5 The Original Houses – architects, builders and design

The new freeholders of the land had next to engage an architect or builder to prepare house and drainage plans for submission to the Wimbledon Local Board together with the Notice of Intended New Buildings. [Plate 6]. The two builders, Townsend and Harmer made their own drawings. Many freeholders took this step quickly, particularly in the 'northern half', i.e. both sides of the road (from No. 7 and No. 22 opposite) up to Southside, Wimbledon Common. Houses then were built from start to finish within the year. On completion, the Wimbledon Local Board Surveyor was required to give a certificate stating that 'the dwelling house erected by . . . described as . . . . is in my opinion in every respect fit for human habitation.'

Architects' or Builders' Drawings in whole or in part had survived in the original until 1981 in the possession of the London Borough of Merton, together with some Notices of Intended Building and correspondence. From these and electoral rolls, some house deeds and some descriptions in Hampton and Sons records, we have been able to establish the pattern and date of events. Present house numbers are used in this study.

We shall now examine the *construction* of the individual buildings, and structural changes to them up to 1983; and the reasons for their form and the accommodation each provided. The various *architects* are dealt with briefly in Appendix III. Seven were Fellows of the Royal Institute of British Architects. Two were Presidents of that body, viz:- Sir Aston Webb [No. 1] and Ernest Newton [No. 7]. Some reference has been made in this Chapter to occupiers, but they are dealt with more fully in Chapters 6 to 11.

There are several contrasts between the *'northern' and 'southern' halves* of the road. The 'northern' houses (apart from No. 4 (1908)) were all built within the two years 1889 and 1890. Apart from the Southside corner houses, none have been converted into leasehold flats. They have remained basically one family houses since they were built.

The houses in the 'southern' half, i.e. both sides of the road (from No. 8 and No. 19 opposite) down to the Ridgway however, were built over a period of ten years from 1889 to 1899. Three of them have passed through periods of non-residential use. These three and one other were later converted into self-contained leasehold flats. Their exteriors have however remained largely unaltered.

There are two semi-exceptions to these patterns. Nos. 7 and 9 were also converted into self-contained flats, but in both the freeholder resides in the ground floor flat, letting the upper two flats furnished. The lets are short-term compared with the leasing unfurnished for 7, 14, or 21 years pattern up to 1939 in some houses of the road.

Three houses in the 'southern' half were architect designed (including the demolished 'Grange Lodge'); the remaining eight designed by the two local builders Townsend and Harmer.   In the 'northern' half, seven were architect designed;   two by a national firm of surveyors; and two by Harmer.   The mystery No. 26 accounts for the twelfth.   The architects did *not* employ Townsend or Harmer to erect their buildings.

Whereas all the houses in the road were *all individual*, they had *in common the features necessary for the social demands of the occupiers of the time.*   In particular should be mentioned, the tradesmen's entrance, coal and wine cellars, domestic offices including pantry, larders, scullery and servants' W.C.   A servants' bathroom and sitting room were often added later (if not originally provided), due to the staff pressures of the time.   In all houses no room used by servants was permitted to overlook the gentry in the garden.

The accommodation on the first and attic floors has only exceptionally been described under the individual houses.   Suffice it to say that usually the first floor comprised three to six gentry bedrooms, bathroom, dressing room, night nursery if required, housemaid's closet, sometimes with 'draw-off' for hot and cold water and linen cupboards.   The attic floor contained from two to five servants' bedrooms, with small iron surround grates, boxrooms and cistern room.

For the owners, day nurseries, studies, libraries were included according to family needs.   Billiard rooms were added later in several properties.   A greenhouse was a 'must' and where space allowed, a tennis lawn.   Motor houses followed mainly in the 1930's to 50's.

The tradesmen called daily to receive the orders, which they then delivered the same day, on credit.

The houses were originally lit by gas (although it is said that No. 26 was lit by oil), and were later converted to electric lighting.   All were at first heated by coal (with the notable exception of 'Grange Lodge' with its hot air central heating).   Heating was later by gas fires in lieu or in addition; still later, electric fires.   Finally central heating by various means, particularly after the road came into the Smokeless Fuel Zone in 1967.

THE 'NORTHERN' HALF OF THE GRANGE
No. 29, The Grange/3 and 3A Southside with No. 27, The Grange
− originally 'Canisbay'
No. 2 Southside/1A, The Grange − 'Grangemuir'
These two properties were built on the 'Southside', corners facing Wimbledon Common.   Their gardens and coach-houses had frontages onto The Grange.   They were and are in cut and moulded brick with decorative plaster work on the top floor facades.   The style is Pont Street Dutch with tiled corner turrets.   Virtually identical, the plans for both were drawn by the still existing firm of surveyors, *Weatherall and Green* of 22 Chancery Lane, W.C.

The reason for these 'twin' houses has not been established since the men for whom they were built were *James R. Malcolm* ('Canisbay') and *Robert T. Thomson* ('Grangemuir'). Were they connected by marriage? Robert Thomson was a ship owner with a City office. James Malcolm was a member of a family firm of jute merchants (William F. Malcolm and Co. of 36, Leadenhall Street). The name 'Canisbay' presumably came from the birthplace of James's wife Erica Whyte; Canisbay, N.E. Caithness, Scotland. The couple subsequently built and went to live in 'Barrogill', and their children and grandchildren in 'Deepdale' and 'Strathrory', all three houses in Calonne Road, Wimbledon.

Now to deal with these two houses individually.

'Grangemuir' (1889) [Plate 7]
Robert Thomson put an engraved stone, which is still there, against the old Lingfield House wall, stating '210 feet of this wall is the property of R. Thomson'. There are plans of two elevations, the ground floor, first floor, second floor and cellar. The outer walls were fourteen inches thick and the interior ones nine inches. The porch positioned as today led to a vestibule with 'a sinking for a mat'. The vestibule led into the hall off which were the dining room and the drawing room both having large bays overlooking Wimbledon Common. As total floor area the drawing room had some 607 square feet! Behind the drawing room was the morning room whose bay looked onto the garden. Beyond the dining room were extensive domestic offices, including butler's pantry, pantry and servery, dressers and cupboards in the kitchen, servants' W.C., and a scullery with a two foot copper washtub. The tradesmen's entrance and the stairs to the cellar (with its wine and coal cellars and larder) led off the kitchen.

This account of the accommodation serves to emphasise the spaciousness of this house, which had ten bedrooms. Thomson had a servants' sittingroom added in 1904. He sold the house to retire to the country in 1909. The purchaser James Unitt Parkes evidently found the 'spaciousness' inadequate and employed an architect, Archibald E. Chasemore of 17 York Place, W. to produce plans for a one-storey billiard room, 22 feet by 26 feet with its own lavatory and W.C. This was built onto the dining room and facing Wimbledon Common with its own bay window. A pantry and maid's room were added as a side extension to the existing scullery, and coach-house cum-stables extended. The original coach-house had rooms over and single floor stabling at the side. The 1909 side-addition provided a coal shed, tool shed and W.C. on the ground floor. Over these and the stable, were built a kitchen, larder and sittingroom for the coachman. The original rooms over the coach-house presumably both became bedrooms. The roof over the smaller building appears to have remained *in situ*. A new roof covering the whole of the extended building was put on top. The harness room was changed into a bathroom in 1946. This apart, the extended building remained structurally unaltered and coach-house doors remained until their replacement in 1978/9 by French doors, and the whole adapted and modernised inside for a private individually owned house (No. 1A The Grange). A 'Motor Garage' (now demolished) was added outside the stable in 1913. In 1910 a conservatory was added to the westside of the main house.

James Parkes died about 1913; his widow let the house and then sold it to Sir William McClintock, a well-known and wealthy accountant, who installed central heating. He, in turn sold the property in the 1920s to John Watts, whose family stayed until war damage in 1944 (cf. Chapter 11). 'Grangemuir' was never again to be a one family house.

An account of the changes to the structure and ownership subsequent to the second war is given in Chapter 11. In spite of the division of the main house into three vertical units the exterior of the building remains much as it was; the chief loss arises from the splitting up of the terrace and large garden at the back on The Grange frontage. Plate 7 gives some idea of how these areas used to look.

'Canisbay' (1889)
The only part of the original plans to have survived is the stabling and coach-house, drawn by Weatherall and Green. These were sited where the present No. 27 The Grange (two self-contained flats, one on each storey) stands. The original coach-house remained in use, latterly as a garage and rooms over, until about 1958 when it was virtually taken down and reconstructed in its present form. It was approached from The Grange by a driveway, opposite that which led to 'Grangemuir' coach-house. It had two horse stalls, a loose box, a harness room and coach-house, and on the floor above, a loft at the front and living and bedroom at the rear, where the stair led up to it. At the front was a 'gully for carriage washing' and a 'manure pit'.

By 1925 the two horse stalls and loose box had been converted to a double garage. The main 1889 house with a billiard room added on the west side about 1909, remained until 1953 much the same sort of family house as described in about 1925 by Hampton and Sons as follows:-

Canisbay
    27 feet x 10 feet Billiards or Dance Room with fireplace in Jacob style.
    3 rec; 3 bath; 11 bedrooms.
    Central heating.
    Double garage and cottage.
    Exceedingly well built and designed, approached by double carriage drive.

Ground Floor — teak floors — vestibule — mahogany doors to recep. rooms, all floored in oak, excellent for entertaining.

Drawing room	25 feet x 22 feet.	Conservatory.
Dining room	27 feet x 22 feet.	
Morning room	20 feet x 15 feet into bay with fitted bookcases in	

recesses.

First Floor — approached by 2 staircases.

1st Bed	22 feet x 21 feet.	Dressing room and bathroom.
2nd Bed	19 feet x 18 feet.	Wash basin and second bath.
3rd Bed	18 feet x 16 feet.	Wash basin.

Another bedroom — now a fitted linen room.

Top Floor 6 good bedrooms — 5 with wash basins. Bathroom and W.C. Housemaids' linen pantry.

G.F. Domestic offices – kit., tiled scullery, fitted independent boiler. Tiled pantry, Servants' sitting room.

Good Cellarage.

Excellent order – Gardens attractively laid out and well stocked. Tennis Lawn.

Garage premises well removed, providing accommodation for 2 cars with 3 living rooms over and bathroom.

'Canisbay' suffered slight war damage in 1944 as did 'Grangemuir'. In 1953 the house was divided vertically into two separate parts; the single storey west side 1909 addition was separated in 1938. These became Nos. 29 The Grange, 3 Southside and 3A Southside (Pond Cottage) respectively.

The very beautfiul wide main staircase and the morning room as described are still in No. 3 Southside, which remained basically a one family house, whereas No. 29 The Grange was converted into a number of small units for letting, the freehold being owned from 1953 mainly by various successive companies. However, in 1982, No. 29 was purchased by the owner of No. 3 Southside, and the whole of the original house has been restored *externally* to its former glory. The loss is its setting, owing to the considerable subdivision of its grounds.

No. 26, The Grange (? early 1889) – originally 'The Grange', then 'Oriel Lodge' from 1891
Mystery surrounds the origins of this house. It is believed to be the first erected in the road, although the surviving partial deeds show that the Conveyance by Sir Richard Mansel Mansel to a *John Cross* did not take place until 27th September 1889. Correspondence between John Cross and the owner of the adjacent 'Canisbay' (which house was not yet completed) in *July* 1889 confirm that Cross was already 'in possession', and support our statement that No.26 was already built. Moreover the partial deeds mention that the house was first called 'The Grange', doubtless in memory of the 18th century house demolished in about 1887. The house in fact passed from John Cross by 1891 into the ownership of *Ernest Constantine Tafel*, retired shipping merchant, who renamed it 'Oriel Lodge'.

No shred of a building plan or letter to the Wimbledon Local Board survives. It is therefore possible, according to the Planning Department of the London Borough of Merton, that the house was erected without permission. Perhaps it would not have passed the statutory requirements. The present owner, an architect, describes the building as having been of a simple design. The 1960s owner maintains that there was originally oil lighting and no bathroom. Thus we guess that the house was designed and erected by a small builder (not Townsend or Harmer).

The house is built in yellow brick with red brick embellishment, and a slate roof. Its porch with front door up a few steps and vestibule faces the road; the tradesmen's entrance being on the north side. At this side at the end of the garden was probably a small building which could have sheltered Mrs. Jessie Tafel's pony and chaise. We believe the elevations to be virtually unaltered. One of the unique features is the Oriel window in the front of the house in the drawing room which also had a window onto the large garden which was mainly at the side of the house.   A small piece of garden was at the rear, but this was extended to the Murray Road frontage in 1905 when the Murray Estate was broken up.   However, part of the old wall between The Grange and Murray Estates remained and still does.   As with other properties on the west side of the road, this extra garden land was later detached from No.26, and a Murray Road house built on it, in 1958.   Part of the garden on the south side was also sold, in 1961 for the building of No. 25, the only infill in the road.

The original Ground Floor rooms of No. 26 seem to have comprised in addition to the drawing room, a dining room at the rear south side with french doors onto the garden, morning room facing the road, with domestic offices at the rear.   The cellarage was under the front of the house with three small rooms presumably for coal, wine or beer and cold larder use.

It is improbable that Mrs. Tafel who was there until her death in 1931, made any major alterations to the original house or indeed that there were any thereafter since it has remained a one family house.   That is of course not to say that improvements were not made internally, so that today it is a charming residence, with modern facilities, whilst retaining one or two original internal features, such as the pine hall screen and the pine balustrade to the staircase.

No. 1, The Grange (1889) [Plate 8] – originally 'Grange Cottage'
This house, the largest in the road, apart from the corner houses, is opposite No.26, and was built on land bought by Peek at the 1888 auction and then sold to *John Franklin Adams* (1843–1912) of Lloyds who engaged *Aston Webb* [see Appendix III] (later Sir Aston) F.R.I.B.A. to prepare the plans.   The house was (strangely, in view of its size) called 'Grange Cottage', perhaps because the name 'The Grange' had already been used by the owner of the slightly earlier No. 26.   It has remained a one-family house.

The house was beautifully built and the elevations today remain unaltered from the date of building, apart from the addition of a billiard room at the rear, probably by Adams' immediate successor, and the usual greenhouse and garages in the grounds. Some of the original signed Aston Webb plans survive, but Hampton and Sons 1930 sale particulars give a good description, as follows:-

Pleasing elevation possessing many unique features having been designed by one of the most eminent architects of his day.
Erected regardless of costs.
Red and brindled bricks with stone enrichments and tiled roof.
Most artistic appearance.   All principal room face south west.
Porch.
G.F.   Vestibule opening into corridor hall, warmed by large stove at foot of main staircase, diffusing warmth throughout the house.   Lavatory and W.C.   Suite of 3 reception rooms 22' x 14', 19' x 14'6", 22' x 14'6", floored in teak parquetry, (3 opening into one another with sliding doors).   Delightful arrangement for entertaining.

G.F. domestic offices.

2 staircases of solid oak to

First Floor 4 beds. Dressing rooms. Separate beds suitable for nurseries.

   3 baths with W.C.s. Heated linen cupboards.

Above 3 maids' bedrooms. Box room, fitted sink etc.

E.L. Joinery exceptional in character. Mahogany doors, Oregon pine panels. Pitch pine flooring. Joinery of oak and teak are exceptionally (fine) and reduce the cost of upkeep to the minimum.

Garden surrounds house and is laid out most skilfully and conveys idea of much larger extent. It includes several fine old trees and a Fives court convertible into a motor garage at small cost.

Nos. 2 and 3 and 24, The Grange
These houses, 2 and 3 being next to each other on the east side, and 24 opposite on the west, were all built to the plans of *Edward J. May, F.R.I.B.A.*, [see Appendix III]. No. 24 had and has a small coach-house, which was built unusually close to the main house and on the same building line for reasons outlined later. All these three houses remain as one family houses.

The land on which Nos. 2 and 3 were to be built had been purchased by Peek and that of No. 24 by Harmer at the 1888 Auction. In each case it was sold to the incoming first occupiers.

No. 2, The Grange (1889) [Plate 9] – originally 'Lyneham', then 'Parham'
Edward May designed and built this house for himself a few months prior to the other two houses. The date is on the arch of the front porch. He lived in the property for some seven years before moving to 23 Spencer Hill, Wimbledon.

The front of the red brick No. 2 as shown in Plate 9 is virtually unaltered from its original form, although May himself extended the dining room, by means of a bay window at the rear of the house, in 1893. In 1894-6 a three storey additional wing at the back was built creating three extra rooms, one on each floor; a rear extension for a new sitting room for the servants and an additional floor over the rear bay window were added in 1924 and 1930 respectively by subsequent owners.

The original front drawing room and first floor main bedroom had windows onto the back garden; these garden views were eliminated by May's new 1894-6 wing. It seems unlikely that May would have altered his original concept of garden views so soon. It may perhaps be assumed that the new owner, William Smith Hastings (then aged about 60) requested him to produce the plans before moving in – possibly to cater for his grandchildren. One of the new rooms on the attic floor was certainly a day nursery.

Then, as today, new owners sought to adapt their 'new' house to suit their own requirements. A relatively modest-sized house was thus enlarged.

No. 3, The Grange (1889)
This next door house was designed by May for his client, *William Joseph Cundell,*

stockbroker.   Like No. 2 the house is of red brick with red tiled roof, and the front elevation basically still as first built.   No substantial alterations or additions have been made to the building, except for an extension to the drawing room in 1923, (by this date at the rear) for the then owner, Mrs. Esmeralda Negroponte.

The ground floor comprised a drawing room on either side of the front door; at the rear a Day Nursery behind the dining room with a bay window onto the garden, a garden door, a W.C. and all domestic offices (pantry, kitchen-store, scullery, servants' W.C. and backdoor).   There was also cellarage.

No. 24, The Grange (1890) – originally 'Fintona', then 'Colebrook', then 'Cedar Lodge'
No. 24 was designed by May in a different style, again with red brick but with a grey slate roof, on a much grander scale, and having its own stable and coach-house.   It was built for *Hugh Pearson Paul*, a ship insurance broker.

May wrote to the Wimbledon Local Board saying 'I have been in special difficulty in arranging the positions of the house and stables on the limited piece of ground, my client making it a necessity to preserve a slip of garden along one side from back to front for the purpose of a single tennis court.'

Correspondence continued and eventually the stable and coach-house instead of being sited on the rear boundary, as would have been usual, as far from the house as possible, were sited to the north on the same building line as the main house.   The rooms over the coach-house were converted into a self-contained 'granny flat' in about 1970, with garage below.

The original front of the house, with its central chimneys, remains, except that a conservatory has been added on the south side.   (? in place of the desired tennis court).   The only other structural addition, was a maid's sittingroom and bathroom at the rear of the domestic offices in 1927.

The following description by Hampton and Sons of the property about 1920 reveals that the garden had been extended by the purchase of land at the back, at the Murray Estate auction of 1905.   Had this land been available when No. 24 was built, no difficulties over the siting of the stabling and coach-house would have arisen.

'Beautiful walled large garden having valuable frontage on Murray Road.
Small kitchen garden.   Summer house; 2 greenhouses.
Perfectly secluded – includes tennis lawn.
Magnificent cedar tree.
3 Recep.; 7 bed and dressing room; 2 bath plus
Stabling with living room over.
Photographic dark room.
G.F. – Hall – fitted fireplace – Cloakroom.
Dining room – 22 feet with square bay x 14 feet going through tiled and heated conservatory to garden.

30

Morning room (front) 14 feet x 12 feet.

Drawing room 22 feet into bay x 21 feet with ingle nook and French windows to back garden.

Domestic offices including pantry, servants' sittingroom and servants' bathroom.

Excellent cellarage.

First Floor — Bedroom 21 feet x 18 feet plus dressing room and bathroom. 2 other good bedrooms. Housemaid's closet and linen cupboard.

Above   — 2 beds, boxroom, loft and tankroom.

Electric light and power.

In 1969 the rear garden was cut back to its original 1890 area, by the sale of the Murray Road frontage land.

No. 23, The Grange (1889) [Plate 10] — originally 'St. Kevin's'
This house stands on a smallish plot originally bought by Harmer at the 1888 auction, then resold to *Mrs. Eliza Blake*, widow, who engaged the architect, *Charles Henry Mileham* [see Appendix III] to produce plans. In 1905 this garden was also extended by purchase of land from the Murray Road frontage. Likewise, this extra land was subsequently resold (in the 1960s), and the area of the property is now as it was when the yellow London brick and red tiled roof house was first built. The exterior walls were 14 inches thick.

The front (N.E. elevation) is little changed, except that over the doorway was the date 1889, and a large capital 'B' (no doubt for Blake) emblazoned over the front attic window. [Plate 10] The known structural additions were the Motor House (since removed) on the south side of the house, and a Conservatory in place of the balcony at the rear; both works were carried out in 1916 on behalf of Dr. John Hayward, the then owner.

In the 'northern' half of the road, this is the only house (aside from the unique semi-detached pair, Nos. 5 and 6) with a semi-basement as distinct from cellarage. The front porch and door is therefore approached up six steps. This semi-basement with its tradesmen's entrance on the north side was described in 1929 in Hampton and Sons brochure as 'Basement — light and cheerful offices comprising range, scullery, capital butler's pantry, sink, cupboards, closet larder, wine and coal cellars. Good servants' hall, W.C. and servants' bathroom and independent boiler for water supply.' The only change from the 1889 plan provisions appears to have been the important addition of the servants' bathroom and the independent boiler.

The main living rooms (drawing room and study/morning room overlooking the garden and the dining room facing the road) had pitch pine floors. The front hall was designed to be room sized and there was (and is) a lift outside the dining room door up from the kitchen regions. At least the servants did not have to run up and down the stairs from the basement with the food they were serving.

No. 4, The Grange (1908) [Plate 11] — originally 'The Little House'
This house, which is opposite No. 23, was the last house to be built. Peek had bought

31

the land at the 1888 auction, then resold it for £300 to George Brown, a land agent living at 'Kingsley', 35 Lingfield Road, whose land abutted onto this plot. He wanted to prevent building at the end of his garden. He did not sell it until some 20 years later. Then *John Archibald Hughes,* printer, acquired it and had his 'Little House' built in 1908 to the plans of the architects *George Hubbard and A.W. Moore* [see Appendix III]. No. 4 was in red brick (now partly pebble dash), with red tiled roof and partially hung tiled with attractive egg and dart moulded friezes. The front door is at the south side of the house, with unusually, the tradesmen's entrance beyond, which led into the usual domestic offices area, but also unusually on this level were the wine and coal cellars.

The front door led into a vestibule with a large hall nowadays closed off with a door, with a front bay window, then through to the inner hall off which led the front drawing room, and at the back, the dining room into which Hughes put a small ingle in 1919. Otherwise the house remains substantially unaltered, and in use as a family house to-day. Plate 11 shows two elevations.

No. 22, The Grange (1890) – originally 'Hawkhurst'
This building has the confirmatory date of 1890 in the brick work below the side chimney stack. It stands on land purchased by Harmer at the 1888 auction; he sold the freehold to *Edward Wilks,* accountant, who commissioned him to design and build the house.

It is built in the yellow London brick which was cheaper than the red brick of the decorative bands. The red tile roof remains, but the original building was smaller than the present one. The front elevation was first altered in 1924 for Mrs. Gwendolyn Nunes, when two new bay windows in the front for the dining room and library, either side of the front door, were inserted, together with the bay windows over for the two front bedrooms and a front dormer window. In 1931 a new bay was put in over the main entrance door. The area between the upper and lower bay windows was then red tile hung, so that the original yellow brick frontage is obscured.

In 1981 an extension at the south side was added, in keeping with the existing brick colours, and size and design of windows on the front elevation, to accord with Mrs. Nunes' house. The plans for this 1981 alteration were drawn by Roland Jovanovic Dip.Ing. Arch. currently living opposite this house.

We believe this house to be the only one in the road, where the *front* elevation is no longer as originally designed.

Nos. 5 and 6, The Grange (1889) [Plate 12]
This is the sole pair of semi-detached villas in the road. They were built and presumed designed by Harmer, (on land acquired from Peek) and are opposite No. 22. Harmer's client was *Mrs. Harriet Gribble* (1807–1892), a widow aged 82, whose reasons for requiring the semi-detached status are told in Chapter 6.

The tall villas (in yellow brick patterned in red brick and with stone surrounded windows) have semi-basements and three storeys above. In each instance the basement comprised the kitchen, scullery, wine cellar and servants' W.C. at the rear of the house, and the larder, coal cellar, and sitting room (15 feet x 14 feet) at the front — presumably for the maids. (These basements have now been converted to units and the main kitchens moved to the first floor). The Ground Floor comprised a lobby and hall, the front sitting room and dining room and a garden door with steps down to the grounds. The elevations remain unaltered.

No. 7, The Grange and its Coach-house (1889) [Plates 13 and 14]
— originally 'Silvertown' — now 'Fralunor'
This property was built on land purchased by *Charles de l'Hoste Holland*, stockbroker, from Peek who bought it at the 1888 auction. The architect was *Ernest Newton F.R.I.B.A.* [see Appendix III]

The house is in red and brindled brick with Broseley red tiles on its pitched roofs, and tile hung to the first floor. The front porch with tile roof and Ionic half pillars on brick walls shelters the front door with brass handles and letterbox. It has many detailed features including the round swing window on the attic floor, the remainder being dormer. The front and side elevations remain as originally designed; and the back as altered in 1903.

The ground floor comprised a gentlemen's lavatory and W.C. near the front door off the vestibule; an inner hall with morning room/study looking onto the road; likewise the drawing room with large bay window with 70 panes of glass. The dining room with a similar bay was at the rear, where there is also a garden door. The first floor rooms over these two also have bays, the bay roofs being covered in lead.

A green baize door led to the butler's pantry, the large kitchen with a range, then through to the scullery (with earthenware sink and teak draining board), marble-shelved larder, servants' W.C., and tradesmen's entrance onto the drive which led up to the coach-house at the bottom of the garden. On the first floor were four large bedrooms, one with a bath en suite. There was also a separate W.C. and the housemaid's closet. On the attic floor were three large bedrooms for servants, a boxroom and a cistern room. The cellars go only under a fraction of the house, nevertheless the coal cellar is large enough to have been used as an air raid shelter in the Second World War, and the wine cellar has stone racks for 350 bottles.

In 1903 Holland again employed Newton to design some additions. An 'extension' wing was built at the back of the kitchen, providing a rearrangement of the domestic offices and a patio, and over this addition, a fifth bedroom or playroom on the first floor, and on the attic floor, an additional boxroom and a re-division to provide four servants' bedrooms.

Interior features include brass stays and handles to the wooden casement windows, brass door knobs and keyhole plates, and decorative brass finger plates to the panelled doors. The brass furniture however, was not supplied in the servants' quarters. A beautiful mahogany banister stair rail with moulded balusters leads right up to the attic floor. Decorative plaster friezes and attractive wooden moulded mantle pieces are in the living rooms. Bell pushes to summon the servants were in the living and bedrooms.

There appears to have been no structural change in the house from 1903 until 1945 when Frank and Lucy Norman converted it into three flats, but not in such a fashion that the flats could be sold as separate leasehold entitities, as they wished to retain internal features, and preserve a one family home aspect.

The original coach-house, stables and rooms over were also built in the same brick with tile hung elevations to first floor level. The interior can be seen from Plate 14. In 1979/81 the coach-house was converted to a five-room 'cottage' to the plans of Norman Plastow, F.R.I.B.A. of Wimbledon. [Plate 15]

This completes the account of the 'northern' half.

'Grange Close', 54 Murray Road (1923)
This house was built between the back gardens of Nos. 19 and 22 The Grange, on the land which extends from The Grange to Murray Road frontages, and was owned by the original owner of No. 7 The Grange. The house is not in the road, and was built to plans by Arthur C. Martin, F.R.I.B.A. of 9 New Square, Lincolns Inn. Since it was not erected until 1923, it is not featured here.

Road Adoption
The slightly earlier 'northern' part of the road, as already defined, was adopted as section I in 1892 by the Wimbledon Local Board, who became responsible for tarmac-adaming the carriage way. The footpath was also to be tarmac with 4 foot slabs. It is interesting to note that at this date three trees were to remain in the carriageway. Doubtless these were the plane tree outside No. 25, the giant holly outside No. 26, and the elm, now unfortunately dead, but the trunk remaining in the pavement out-side No. 7.

Section II of the road, i.e. the 'southern' part, as already defined, was not adopted until some five years later i.e. in 1897.

THE 'SOUTHERN' HALF OF THE GRANGE
Although we have dealt with the 'northern' half of the road by way of houses opposite to each other, it makes sense to deal with each side of the 'southern' half separately, Nos. 8 - 12 on the east side of the road having been built by Townsend on land bought by him, and Nos. 15 - 19 on the west on Harmer's. Two were built by him, and three by others. Townsend's were built in the following order:- Nos. 9. 12, 8, 11, and 10.

No. 8, The Grange (1889) [Plate 16] – originally (and still) 'Whyteleafe'
This, the only one family *house* retaining its original name, was built on several auction lots (probably three). Townsend sold the freehold land to, and his firm Parsons, Townsend and Son was commissioned to build the house for, *Henry Warlters Horne*, a barrister.

34

This substantial construction, built in red brick, has scalloped hung tiles to first floor level, and tile roof; also several interesting decorative features, including fancy ridge tiles and patterned red brick work round the ground floor windows [Plate 16]. The site plan shows the *Sheep Walk*, residents or landowners at the rear in Lingfield Road, and the already built Nos. 7 and 9 The Grange on either side of No. 8. It also makes clear that the building was placed near No. 9, virtually all the garden being on the north side, to provide for the tennis court area. The carriage way was a short sweep to and round the north side of the house to the back. The ground floor contained the large vestibule from a porchway; spacious hall and gentlemen's cloakroom; smoking room (later called the morning room or study), all on the road front. The dining room had windows both on the road, and on the garden. Pantry, kitchen and scullery were at the south rear.

Horne made alterations to the domestic offices area in 1903, expanding them to include W.C.s and a 'Cycles and Work Room', and the pantry was made to double as a servants' sittingroom. At the same time, greater use was made of the original basement area, which had only contained coal and wine cellars and a larder. One new basement room was marked 'Boots'. These alterations were to the plans of Thomson and Pomeroy, architects and surveyors of 49, Hill Road, Wimbledon. *Robert J. Thomson, F.R.I.B.A. (1864-1937),* who designed a number of works in Wimbledon was the son of the Woodside nursery gardens Thomson, and father of David Thomson, who died in 1978 at the house opposite, No. 17. The occupier after Horne was Colonel John Winn.

The house remained substantially unaltered until 1948 when the then owner, Commander A.M.C. Stileman and Mrs. Evelyn Stileman (the daughter of Colonel Winn) converted it into four flats, (two or three of them remaining for the extended family however). The top floor was let from about 1950 to 1972, to Dr. and Mrs. Douglas Gibson, but the house has now in effect become a one family house again for later generations of Stilemans.

Nos. 9, 10, 11 and 12, The Grange
Townsend gave Notice of Intention to build four houses in January 1889. In the event only Nos. 9 and 12 were built in 1889, and fresh notices for Nos. 10 and 11 were submitted in 1891.

No. 9, The Grange (1889) [Plate 17] – originally 'Eversley'
This house was designed and built by Townsend on his own freehold land. It seems to have been completed before his houses on either side (Nos. 8 and 10). He continued as freeholder for some years, renting it out in the first place to *Henry Eugene Tracey* for seven years. The succeeding occupier, *Mrs. Elizabeth Lee*, widow, as sitting tenant, bought the freehold from Townsend in about 1897. She remained at No. 9 until her death in 1922.

The house is built in red brick with scalloped hung tiles, and tiled roof. The garden is mainly on the south side of the house. The front and side elevations are reproduced. [Plate 17]. Various ornamental features appear on the front elevation

which remains as in 1889.   The front porch and door are shown at the Common side
of the house, (and so remain as the front door to the ground floor flat.)

The library and drawing room (also with bay overlooking the garden) faced the road.
Behind it the dining room, also with a side garden view, but the kitchen and scullery
at the rear of the library had no outlook.   Below them in the basement were coal and
wine cellars and larder and pantry.

In April 1902, a plan was produced for Mrs. Lee by Edwin Hill, builder, of 26 West
Place, Wimbledon Common, which extended the kitchen to fill the area behind the
original drawing room.   Since the latter would no longer have a window looking to the
back, a new bay window (9'6" x 6'0") was inserted on the garden side overlooking the
lawn, which was 50 feet wide.   It is interesting that the lawn width alone was the
frontage representing *one* auction lot.

The property appears to have remained unaltered thereafter until October 1945 when
an application by Dr. J. Nairn Dobbie (who had bought the house at Mrs. Lee's death
in 1922) was granted to convert the house into three flats (one on each floor).   He
and his wife Joan remained in one of the flats until 1951.

A planning proposal for an infill of a small house on the garden of No. 9 was refused in
1957 as it would have created too intensive a use of the site.   In 1962 the new owner
was granted permission to convert the ground floor flat into two, and add further
garages at the back.   She lives in the front (larger) ground floor flat herself and is the
freehold owner and occupier.   The entry to the upper flats is at the beautiful garden
side but neatly concealed next to her conservatory.   The elevations are therefore
virtually unchanged, from 1902 at least.

No. 10, The Grange (1891) [Plate 18]
This was another Townsend house designed and erected by him, on some of his freehold land (90 feet frontage), for leasing out.   Since it was not built for an owner
occupier, no alterations seem to have been made until he sold the freehold to the
sitting tenant, *John Curzon Ingle*, solicitor, in 1905.   An example of a 21 years leasehold agreement survives for this house.   The front elevation remains as originally
designed, as does the front porch and door on the north side.   The house is in red
brick, with decorative white patterning, and roof covered with board, felt and tiles and
fancy ridge tiles.

Entering into the spacious tiled hall with fireplace, the gentlemen's cloakroom
(lavatory and separate W.C.) is immediately on the right.   The lavatory still contains
the original tip-up pedestal basin in white china with markings to resemble marble.
There are also brass taps.   The *'Lift-Up' patent* was granted to George Jennings, Palace
Wharf, Stangate, Lambeth.   The front rooms were the morning room, and the drawing
room with window onto the garden, laid out at the south mainly as a tennis lawn, at
least by 1905.   The dining room with large bay window was at the south side; the
scullery, kitchen and pantry at the rear.

In the semi-basement, the servants' hall was at the back with area window onto the

36

drive.   The larder, wine and coal cellars were along this side also.   The design of the coal cellar (12 feet x 18 feet) seems unusual on two counts.   First, the coal chute is at the front of the house, under the morning room window, and secondly the servants' W.C. was placed in the front corner of the coal cellar.   [Plate 18]

In 1912, Ingle added a new room, a large study with bay at the southern side of the house, linked by a lobby to the original living room; a conservatory at the rear of the study was also built.   The study was said to be needed so that the head of the household should not be disturbed by his daughters arriving home late.   One wonders if it was also to distance himself from the room farthest away, by then used as a drawing room where his elegant wife had her musical evenings.

Although internal partitioning was done in 1950 by Mrs. Vera Armitage who bought the property on Widow Ingle's death, the house was reconverted to much its 1912 form as a one family house when its present owner bought it in 1960.

11, The Grange (1891)
This was the other house designed and built by Townsend in 1891 for leasing.   The material used was again red brick with tile roof and decorative ridge tiles in different patterns from No. 10.   The drawings show a virtually identical ground floor plan with entrance at the side, and the rooms as described for No. 10.   At some later point the entrance door seems to have been moved to the front of the house, through what had been the gentlemen's cloakroom.

The attic floor with four or five bedrooms was also identical, but the first floor had a fifth bedroom and dressing room at the back.   Although the area, approximately half the house from front to back, occupied by the basement rooms was the same as No. 10, in this house the coal cellar with its chute (sometimes marked 'shoot') down from the drive is at the back of the house where No. 10's servants' hall was; the wine cellar and larder in the middle at the front (where No. 10's coal cellar is) is a room marked 'beer', and it is in this that the servants' W.C. is more suitably situated.   Was the *beer cellar* also the servants' hall?

No alterations (other than the change of situation of the front door) occurred until plans were submitted in July 1939 by a Mrs. Boag, for conversion of the house into two maisonettes forming what are now Nos. 11 and 11A.   The house was split horizontally; the basement and ground floor form one maisonette with the early front door; and the first and attic floors the other, reached by a new set of outside steps on the south of the house up to their front door on a level below the first floor; then inside up by the original stairs to the attic floor.   Appropriate internal alterations were made.   The house remains as maisonettes today.

It is rumoured that Townsend built the house for a daughter on her marriage.   However none of the family lived there according to the electoral rolls.   It seems more likely that he did not sell the freehold of this house to any sitting tenant, but that his eldest daughter Frances Sophia (born 1854) who married a Reverend George Boag, inherited it on her father's death in 1917.   Boag is an unusual name, so we surmise

37

that the Mrs. Boag who had the conversion to maisonettes carried out in 1939 was indeed Frances Sophia, although by then aged 85. In fact she survived until 1949. It looks as if the Townsend family retained this freehold until at least 1939.

No. 12, The Grange / 38 Ridgway (1889)
— originally 'Laughton' and 'Grangeside'
These were also built by Townsend as a *pair* of houses, but joined together from south to north, as can be seen from the Ridgway side. The materials are red brick with hung tiles, some of them scalloped. There are many other decorative features and large stone mullion windows. The elevations are unaltered apart from garage and greenhouse extensions. Each half of the house had its own entrance porch in the appropriate road; the rooms in each half were identical in size and number, but transposed in aspect. Thus, the drawing room of No. 12 faces south; that of No. 38 north onto the gardens. A hall, library, dining room and cloakroom were also provided on the ground floor. Unlike Townsend's other houses, the basements extended over the full area beneath the ground floor; indeed were semi-basements as the front doors have to be reached by steps. Each basement contained a large kitchen, pantry, scullery, larder, wine and coal cellars and W.C. In both houses there were three bedrooms and a bathroom on the first floor, and three bedrooms and a large cistern room in the attic.

The first lessee of No. 12 was *Amy Lee*, a widow, who at some point purchased the freehold from Townsend. She remained at No. 12 until her death in 1920 when the freehold was sold to George Coulter.

The freehold of No. 38 Ridgway however, certainly remained with Townsend, (the rent in 1904 was £130), who left it in his will to another daughter, Mary Ellis Townsend. She died in 1918, only a year after her father. Thitherto the house was leased variously as a one family house. It remained leased until 1942 when the Moldaus purchased the freeholds of both No. 12 The Grange (from Widow Coulter) and No. 38 Ridgway. In 1951 they obtained permission to knock through the stone dividing wall to incorporate two extra bedrooms into No. 12 in which they lived. In the interim they had sold No. 38, which was converted into flats, but later purchased the freehold. Both freeholds still belong to the same occupier at No. 12.

'Grange Lodge' (sometimes numbered 13, sometimes 14), The Grange (1890)
[Plates 19 and 20]
This is the only original building in the road which is no longer standing. It was situated on the corner of Ridgway, with a frontage of 145 feet on The Grange. The plans were drawn up by the architects, *John Thomas Wimperis and William Arber* [see Appendix III]. Their client was *Sir Joseph Bazalgette, C.B.*, the eminent engineer, of whom and his daughter Theresa for whom he had the house built, we write in Chapter 11. The March 1890 plans of the south elevation [Plate 19] give some indication of the size and splendour of this outsize house. The plans show the front entrance and porch with rounded arch which was to have faced The Grange, with a circular drive in front. Sir Joseph changed his mind, and after a struggle with the local Board, got an amended plan passed providing for the carriage drive and front porch to be on the north side. The coach-house, stable block and stable court were beyond the carriage drive entrance court. Perhaps unusually at that date the coach-house had

revolving shutter doors. A weather cock was over the hay loft. By 1929 the coach-house had gone. Both for the main house and the coach-house a complete set of plans survive. Plate [20] shows the rooms on the ground floor with the large conservatory. The basement extended under the whole of the ground floor, and included the kitchen, scullery, butler's pantry, servants' hall and usual store, larder, beer and wine cellars.

The heating chamber was unique, and was to provide some sort of hot air cental heating. There appear to have been no coal fireplaces in the main rooms. Sir Joseph had probably also installed electricity from the outset. On the first floor were three large bedrooms, two with dressing rooms attached, and a large bathroom with separate W.C. The attic floor, reached by the *back stairs*, had four servants' bedrooms, a linen room, and a housemaid's service closet, together with the large cistern room. The exterior walls of the house were 16 inches thick, and the interior walls 9 inches. The garden lay mainly along the Ridgway frontage.

After Miss Bazalgette died in 1922, the new owner had plans drawn in 1923 by the architects Nicholls Hughes for some relatively minor internal alterations, apart from a bathroom in the basement and one on the attic floor, both obviously for the servants; that on the top floor for the housekeeper only, and the basement one for the maids.

In 1935, another owner was not permitted to convert the property into three self-contained flats. Would that he (Mr. Endacott) had succeeded in his application, as the building would almost certainly never have been demolished. By 1938, the house had become Grange Lodge Hotel, and remained as such until 1959, when it and the splendours of Bazalgette's fine house were demolished, to be replaced, ready for occupation in 1961, by the modern block of leasehold flats which stands there to-day.

No. 15, The Grange (1899) [Plate 21] – originally 'Oakley'
This red brick house with tiled roof and unusual chimney stacks was designed by *Richard Creed, F.R.I.B.A.* [see Appendix III]. It is built on *two* auction plots of land, purchased by Harmer at the 1888 auction, but not apparently used by him, until his sale of the land for this house some ten years later. In the meantime 'Grange Lodge' and 'Ingleside' (No. 16) on either side were already built.

Creed seems to have experienced difficulty with the Wimbledon Urban District Council, to whom he had submitted his Notice of Intention in January 1899, since he writes on 6th February to say 'the land at the side (south) of the proposed House is required for a lawn tennis Court and the principal rooms of the house front onto this. I do not see how another could be built upon this land without spoiling the proposed one, and I undertake not to build a second house on this land.' This apparently satisfied the planning authority, and building proceeded.

The house was purpose designed for *Mrs. Ellen Jackson*, widow, and her two children, Ethel and Lionel, then aged about 17 and 6 respectively. Creed was a Trustee under her solicitor husband, Arthur Percy Jackson's will, he having died in 1896 aged 39. There is a stone in the wall of the house saying 'Ethel and Lionel laid me in 1899'.

The front porch faced The Grange (now the entry to the ground floor flat only) and the tradesmen's back entrance on the same north side of the house (now the entry for Flats 3 and 4). The ground floor had a lobby, lavatory with W.C., a hall, drawing room with bay onto the garden, dining room, and at the rear, kitchen, pantry, scullery with servants' W.C. and a 'day larder'. Stairs led from this larder to the cellarage for coal, wine and large larder. The equivalent larderage to-day is a 'fridge' in the kitchen and a 'deep freeze' in the cellar.

The night nursery and a 'playroom' for Lionel proved useful later for Ethel's two children, born as Fordes in 1906 and 1908 at No. 15. The Fordes went later to live at No. 49 Murray Road, almost due west from No. 15 The Grange.

After Mrs. Jackson's death in 1913, her children let the house and then sold it in 1920. It was resold in 1924 to William Latchford (timber merchant) who had alterations carried out to the plans of S. B. Pritlove, architect. Apart from changing the situation of the staircase from the ground floor to the first, and throwing the playroom and linen room into one as a large bedroom, the main change was on the attic floor. The roof space on the second floor was further used, and the whole area converted to provide three bedrooms, sitting room, kitchen, bathroom and separate W.C. The original elevations remain.

We were told that shortly after William Latchford's death, his widow and son nearly sold the property to a pig farmer. His pigs died of swine fever at the last minute. He went bankrupt and withdrew from the sale, but surrendered the plans he had already had drawn up for the conversion of the house into four self-contained units. The conversion was then carried out for Mrs. Latchford in 1954, and she continued to live in one of the flats, selling the others leasehold. She made a covenant with the other three leasehold owners relating to the maintenance and repair of the outside of the house, and insurance, and to the appointment of a surveyor to arrange any necessary outside works.

Mrs. Latchford sold her own Flat 4 in 1962, but the property still remains under the covenant as described. This was the first instance of such an arrangement in the road, though similar covenants were later made in connection with Nos. 16, 17, and 18, which are the only examples of conversions into owner-occupied leasehold flats. These four houses are adjacent to each other.

No. 16, The Grange (1897) – originally 'Ingleside'
This house is built in red with tiled roof, fancy chimney pots, scalloped hung tiles over roof windows, and stone surrounds to the lower windows.

Harmer had bought the land on which No. 16 stands, but having sold the freehold of a plot on the north side for No. 17, and the land to the south being still unsold, he appears to have decided to submit plans himself, and erected this house in 1897. This he leased out for a good many years, until selling the freehold to the sitting tenant, *Sir Sydney Hoare* in 1917. Hoare had lived there since 1906.

The ground floor had the usual drawing room, dining room, study, with at the north side, kitchen, scullery, pantry, store and gentlemen's cloakroom. Below under half the house was the cellarage for coal, wine, larder and servants' W.C. By 1903 at least, the hall was heated by a Hot Water Coil.

The house elevations remain much the same today, though as a result of events following the departure of the second freeholder, the Reverend and Mrs. Frederick Williams in 1938/39, the house was never again to be a one family house. The same applies to Nos. 17 and 18.

From September 1939 to March 1946, the house was leased as offices by the National Mutual Life Association of Australasia Ltd. (previously of 5 Cheapside), with a resident caretaker and his wife. Few internal alterations were made at this stage. Wimbledon Corporation consent for office usage had been granted for the duration of the war and a reasonable time thereafter, provided the property be then vacated and restored to its proper use as a dwelling house.

On the company's release of the property shortly after the end of the war, the Wimbledon Corporation compulsorily purchased the house and converted it into three flats for Council rehousing purposes limited to a period of ten years to May 1957. The Council tenants remained until 1956, when the local authority sold the freehold to a businessman, who obtained permission to retain the existing use as three self-contained flats on a permanent basis. He never lived there but sold the flats on 999 year leaseholds in 1957 and 1958. Shortly afterwards he sold the freehold of the whole property to the 1957 leaseholder of Flat 1. That person on leaving in 1960, sold the freehold to the leaseholder of Flat 3, Mrs. Alice Dodwell, widow. She in her turn left the road in 1966, but she took the freehold with her. However, after her death in 1980, her son sold it to the company that was formed by the three current leaseholders.

Thus this house was brought into line with most of such of the other original houses which have been converted into self-contained flats, whereby the freeholders are also occupiers of part of the house.

Whereas in all other instances, the cellars form part of the ground floor flats, those of No. 16 are shared, entry being from outside the building.

No. 17, The Grange (1893) − originally 'Pendreath' then 'Abingdon'
This house also was built on part of the land acquired by Harmer at the 1888 auction. Here again he apparently took no further steps for some years; then sold the plot(s) to *Miss Wilhemina Bushby Harkness* of Torquay in January 1893 for £720. The architect she commissioned was *Richard Creed* F.R.I.B.A. The connection between the Jacksons of No. 15, and Miss Harkness will be explained in Chapter 6. The house is in yellow brick, red tile hung to the first floor.

The porch and front entrance was at the south side, leading to a vestibule, lavatory and hall, with the smoking room and drawing room facing onto the road. The dining room was behind the drawing room, facing the garden. The domestic quarters at the back also projected some 18 feet further into the garden area than the dining room

41

windows. They included a tradesmen's entrance, stores, larder, kitchen, scullery and from the start, a servants' sitting room. The 'small' cellar under the house merely provided for coal, wine, and beer.

When Miss Harkness moved from No.17 in 1900, taking her house name 'Pendreath' with her it was renamed 'Abingdon' by the new owner, J.B. Bull, who paid £3400 for the house and land. The house remained a one family house until into the Second World War, when the Wimbledon Corporation requisitioned it, at a 'compensation' rental of £150 per annum, and adapted it for occupation by various sets of Council tenants on each floor. The Corporation purchased the house in 1959 from the absentee freeholder, (who had bought the freehold in 1950). Within two years the Corporation sold it to a development company, General Freeholds Limited. This firm did a 'proper' conversion, and then sold the three self contained units as leasehold flats (one on each floor). There was little structural change. The tradesmens' entrance door serves as the front door to the Ground Floor flat, and the main original front door leads to the First and Top Floor flats up the original staircase (now enclosed).

David Thomson, already referred to in connection with No. 8, bought the ground floor flat leasehold in 1965, and then in 1967 the freehold of the whole house, thus setting the trend for one of the owners of a leasehold flat in a converted house, being also the freeholder.

No. 18, Grange Road (1893) [Plate 22]

This land had also been purchased by Harmer at the 1888 auction but left vacant, until he conveyed it on 12 December 1892 to *Arthur Cawston*, architect, (1857–94) [see Appendix III], who submitted his plans to the Local Board in August 1893. He can only just have moved into the completed house when he died aged 37 on 8th June 1894, leaving his widow Evelina Alice to reside there for some ten years. Thereafter she leased it to two successive families, before finally selling in 1921.

The house was built in red brick with red tile roof. Many of the houses in the road have steeply pitched roofs, but this one is extremely long and steep, with fancy ridge tiles and a weather vane over the top dormer window. The building is therefore taller than those on either side (17 and 19), both of which were built slightly earlier.

The account from Hazel Jackson, who lived there in the 1920s and '30s, together with our visit to the house as at present, has enabled us to piece the picture together. The front and side elevations remain basically as originally. The front entrance led into a vestibule and hall running through to the back, where there was a garden door, with cloakroom adjacent. A very beautiful staircase led from the hall. The kitchen, scullery, pantry and tradesmen's entrance were on the north rear of the house at the back·of the front dining room. The morning room and drawing room with large bow window faced somewhat surprisingly onto the blank north wall of No. 17, which was already erected. However the now combined morning and drawing room is both beautiful and pleasant.

The basement is extensive, and must have contained not only the coal and wine cellars, and larder with marble shelves, but also a servants' sitting room lit by an 'area' window. At some point a 'photographic dark room' was put in the house; perhaps this was also in the basement.

The house remained a one family house until the Second World War, without structural alterations, until the property was bought by the Constructional Engineering Union as wartime offices on the ground floor, with living accommodation above for the General Secretary, John Stanley and his relatives. Internal alterations were obviously made. The final outcome of the later history of the house saw its emergence into its present form of five leasehold flats, with the ground floor leaseholder being also the freeholder, and a company formed of the leaseholders to maintain the external fabric. The only major change of elevation from the original building was the addition of the ugly iron staircase at the rear leading to the upper flats.

No. 19, The Grange (1892) – originally 'Wolstan'
The land on which this house was built was also purchased by Harmer at the 1888 auction and likewise remained vacant for some years. The house was built specifically for *George Dixey*, chartered accountant; the plans could have been drawn by an architect, but there is nothing on them, except Harmer's stamp. In the absence of other evidence, no deeds being available either, we must assume that Harmer sold the land freehold to George Dixey, who requested him to plan and erect No.19. The Notice of Intended New Buildings was submitted to the Wimbledon Board by Harmer on 17th. February 1892.

This compact house is in red and yellow brick, with tiled roof and a turret at the east corner. The confirmatory date of 1892 can be seen on the south side of the building. The drawings show the porch and front door at the south side of the house, as today, with the drawing room with bay, and the dining room on the turret side, both facing the road front. The library was at the back, and the domestic quarters and tradesmen's entrance on the northern side of the house. Below this back part of the house were two coal cellars, one for house coal and one for kitchen coal. (There were fireplaces in every room.) In addition there were the larder with marble shelves, a wine cellar with wooden bottle racks, and another store room. The elevations remain virtually unaltered today, apart from the conversion of a central front window into french doors, and the addition of a conservatory at the rear. Various internal changes have been made, but the house has remained as family accommodation throughout its existence.

Thus the account of the 'southern' half of the road is complete.

6. The First Occupiers, 1889 – 1900

Who were the first owners/leaseholders? All properties in the road were *houses*, designed for occupation by families with at least two servants; often with up to four. No *flats*; though since 1945 several houses have been *converted* into self-contained flats; and one was demolished, in favour of a three storey block of twelve flats. Two of the original properties were built as semi-detached; but these were more sizeable than what people are familiar with as the typical inter-war and post-1945 semi-detached construction. Five houses had detached coach-houses, accommodating a carriage, a couple of horses or more, the coachman, with sometimes his family. Each house had its own garden, of perhaps a half to three-quarters of an acre.

The types of property determined, and were determined by, the first occupiers. Some were built to the command of the occupiers, themselves pre-determined; others with a specific occupier-designate and his/her needs in mind; others, still, the so-called speculative builders' productions, with only one point less of specificity in response to anticipation of demand. In Chapter 5, we have indicated in what proportions the properties may be classified. In this chapter, we need to emphasize that with The Grange overall, the extent of specifcity was far greater than for most housing property created at that period; it seems also to have been so, even in comparison with the other middle class housing in Britain.

F.M.L. Thompson in his massive history of Hampstead, called the phenomenon 'droves of widows' This matches our findings in The Grange. Hampstead and North Wimbledon were not exceptional in this. In Glasgow a quarter of the households were 'headed by widows *or spinsters*, and the proportion was similar in the other places' (Exeter, Leamington Spa, The Park Estate, Nottingham, and Sheffield). Of the 24 original occupiers in the road heads of households, seven were merchants or otherwise in business, i.e. just under a third. Seven were members of the professions, i.e. just over a quarter. Two of unknown occupation; William Smith Hastings of No. 2, but see below, and Crawhall of No. 11. Nine, more than the number of merchant/ businessmen, *were either widows or spinsters*. Seven of the women were widows. Apparently, being the widow of a middle class man from 1871 onwards was the best means of achieving property and personality in middle class suburban terms; being a spinster, preferably with well-off widow-women attached, bound to precede you into the next world, was the next best bet.

That lasted till 1900. Between 1900 and 1914, other classifications appeared as most favourable for those aspiring to comfort in suburbia. We shall define them later. *Middle class* Britain, in its own way, must have been almost as rough and tough a prelude to future life as *working class* Britain *up to 1900*. Few now would dispute the toughness and roughness of the latter experience. If one survived the latter, it was a near-miracle. If one survived the former, one was well placed.

Taking the women first, Bazalgette, Beattie, Blake, Cox, Harkness, Gribble, Jackson and the two Lees, we find the following personalia. In No. 5 (and No. 6, which she owned but leased out) (i) Widow Harriet Gribble, with whom we deal later. (ii) Widow Elizabeth Lee — Lee 'Eversley' — as the Stilemans of No. 8 called the occupier of No. 9, the property next door to theirs to the south. (iii) The Coxes, spinsters, had No. 11 around the turn of the century. (iv) Miss Tissie Bazalgette had 'Grange Lodge' which we shall be dealing with in Chapter 11. (v) Widow Ellen Jackson, in No. 15, with two children, who were taken up as god-children of Miss Wilhemina Harkness, spinster, of No. 17. Miss Harkness left a will which we found particularly revealing. (vi) Mrs. Alice J. Beattie, of No. 16 was, presumably, another widow. The house was not built till 1899. (vii) Mrs. Eliza Maria de Vitre Blake, widow, of No. 23, had most of her children in Bombay. It was therefore specially difficult to trace her background, although they lived in Lansdowne Road, Wimbledon, before moving to The Grange. We now have seen Mrs Beattie's and Anna Cox's wills.

The reader will appreciate the variety presented by the *women*, detached from men (as distinct from wives and daughters) in the 1889 to 1900 group. Again, using the Stileman code-language classification, there was Lee, 'Laughton'. Amy, widow, who lived at No. 12, which was involved over the generations with No. 38, Ridgway, another bit of Townsend's North Wimbledon speculative building creations.

It would be misleading to leave the women thus, as in their own right. We should remember that for most of the working part of each day, *all* properties in the road, were *for all practical purposes* women-controlled, whether or not their ownership was nominally with their husband or some other male head of household. So they have *remained*, throughout their existence of nearly a century. We shall be presenting our data relating to the twentieth century in subsequent chapters. Here, we need only make the general point that, from its beginning, our road has been dominated *not* by males but by females.

For lack of space we cannot present our data *descriptively*. But we should put life into some of the *dramatis personae* whom we have hitherto presented as backing to our analysis. *First*, we take one of the *spinsters*. Miss Mary Cox is shown in the electoral registers, Trim's directory, and a lease and site-plan dated St. Valentine's Day, 1895, and in Kelly's directory well on into the first World War, as *occupier* of No. 11, joined, in 1908, by Miss Anna Cox, presumably a sister.

Second, we present one of the most comfortably off of the spinsters, Miss Wilhemina Bushby Harkness of No. 17, the house she first had built, then, called 'Pendreath'. This name she bestowed in turn on the house she moved to some seven years later, where she died, in Clifton Road, three roads further west. Her Torquay home had also been 'Pendreath'.

It was not uncommon, in that epoch, for men and women, never previously married, to marry in middle or later life. But Miss Harkness stayed single till the end in 1905, when she was 63. Women who were past bestowing their hand, were yet acute in bestowing their property. Their last will and testament, in such circumstances,

45

represents the best single source of information about their character and life.

Miss Harkness made her will on 17th March, 1903 and died in 1905. Her main legacies were to the three daughters of her brother William, living in New South Wales, £10,000 in equal shares. Small legacies went to twenty other individuals. These included Ellen Jackson, her friend of No. 15, The Grange, widow, who had come there in 1899 with her two children, Gwendoline Ethel and Lionel Boys Cameron Jackson, whom Miss Harkness numbered by 1903 among her god-children. Among the beneficiaries, also, were several servants: — Janet Elizabeth Adam (probably her house-keeper) an annuity of £50; Jane Sillars (perhaps her personal maid or cook) an annuity of £10; William Pink 'if in my service at my death, £25' (probably her butler/gardener); 'and to each of my maid servants who shall have been with me more than 12 months at the date of my death, legacies of £5 each'. The residue was left to Thomas George, another of her brothers, whom she appointed as one of her two executors and trustees, during his life and after his death to his wife Augusta Helene Harkness. . . and to their children thereafter. If none such, and after giving conditional rights to her trust estate to various nephews and nieces and the Jackson boy, then to the Paddington Green Children's Hospital and/or the East London Hospital for children, Shadwell.

The widows, to whom we now come, must be sub-classified into two types. Gribble and Blake had some grown-up children living with them. Amy and Elizabeth Lee each lived with companions. For our *third* instance, we examine Widow Gribble. She had lived previously in Homefield Road, two roads further east, closer to Wimbledon High Street. As already explained, Harmer built for the 82 year old Mrs. Gribble the semi-detached pair of houses at Nos. 5 and 6 The Grange. Mrs. Gribble's husband Thomas, merchant, died 35 years earlier, eight years after a spell of three years in Lima, Peru. Two of their daughters were born in Lima. In all, five spinster Gribble daughters all in their forties and fifties, lived with their mother and moved to The Grange. Widow Gribble's one son, was the youngest child Henry Edward, solicitor, was already married, living at 3 Thornton Hill, Wimbledon, with children of his own, and practising in London.

Mrs. Gribble's will, dated 14th. June 1886, came into effect on her demise in 1892. It showed she had inherited from her late father £2,000 for her life and after her death for her children as she might direct. She appointed it should pass to her 'dear daughters' equally. 'My. . . son has been advanced by me in life and a proportion of my property is charged with the payment of £1,500 advanced and lent by me to him, and I have further advanced and lent him £2,000. . . I expressly declare that the appointment of my son as one of my executors shall in no way release him from the obligation of the said bond'; 'I bequeath to my son the picture of 'The Repulse' now hanging in my dining room'. One possibility of the provenance of this - somewhat unexpected possession — is that Widow Gribble was given it by her near neighbour in Homefield Road, Sir Thomas Wilmot Peregrine Blomefield Bt.. In her final years, while she owned this prized picture, they were even closer, in fact *next-door* neighbours. Blomefield came from No. 19, Homefield Road, to become Widow Gribble's leasehold tenant in No. 6, The Grange in 1890; simultaneously with Mrs. Gribble's moving from No. 27, Homefield Road into No. 5, The Grange. Another reason for linking the picture with Blomefield was that his baronetcy dated from his naval ancestor's connection with the Battle of Copenhagen in the earlier phase of the Revolutionary and Napoleonic wars with France.

Widdow Gribble may have been trying to get her only son involved with responsibility for all or at least some of his spinster sisters, from some time before his mother made her will in 1886. He took her loans but repulsed her suggestions that he accept other responsibilities than to repay them on a purely financial basis. She may still have been hoping, when she got Henry Harmer to build the semi-detached pair of houses at Nos. 5 and 6, The Grange, in 1889, that her son, Henry Edward, would come with his family to live in one of the pair, thus through property and proximity again to become more involved. Her wiles did not work ten years before her death; nor her wiles with variations three years before her death. She felt sufficiently hopeless that they would; so wrote him out of her unchanged will as early as 1886, but wrote him *into it* by a legacy which should be interpreted as a barbed pun. Money was powerful; but not all-powerful. Poor widow-women had few weapons; this one proved a damp squib.

From what we have been able to glean of the subsequent fortunes of her five lorn girls, as perhaps she thought of them, she need not have worried so much. The eldest, Marian Harriet, died no more than five years after her mother, in 1897, when she was only 59. The youngest, Ellen died in 1910 aged 65, and Agnes in 1914 at 73. The remaining two sisters Catherine and Beatrice lived on at No. 5 until 1925 and 1926, when one was 82, and the other 86. But their equally spinster nieces, Katherine and Harriet Emily, part of the offspring of Widow Gribble's recalcitrant son, were granted probate to their spinster aunts' wills. One of the nieces, Katherine, was a member of the Wimbledon Literary and Scientific Society, aged 38 at the time when she was granted probate in respect of the estate of her namesake aunt in 1926. No. 5 remained with the Gribbles to that year. The money continued in the family, which stayed in the same marital condition. Henry Edward seems to have been the exception to the norm for this intensely female family. *He* died in 1909 at the age of 63, leaving four of his five sisters still surviving, and a son also carrying on as a solicitor.

So much for the women of 1889 to 1900, so important a social feature in our road.

We now turn to an analysis of the early occupiers by socio-economic class of heads of household. The next biggest group among the original occupiers, after the women, were the merchants/other businessmen; a third of the whole. Samuel Smiles' 'Thrift' presented entrepreneurs and engineers as *the* mainspring of the Victorian middle class. In *our* bourgeois road, coming into being in the 1890s, they did *not* outweigh in over-all numbers, nor out-face in its total complexion, this middle class society in embryo. We have seen how Mrs. Gribble, and we shall see how Mrs. Tafel of No. 26, widows, derived their ability to buy or maintain properties in the road from having merchant husbands. But we may note that Mrs. Cawston (No. 18) was an architect's widow; that one of Miss Harkness' executors was a colonel; and that Widow Gribble's son was a solicitor. The merchants/other businessmen do not seem to have made any special local display of greater wealth and power than did the women; nor the professionals who were the other most numerous group of male heads of households among the original occupiers. To review them:— Robert Templar Thomson of 'Grangemuir' was a shipowner; John Franklin Adams of No. 1, occupied a senior position at Lloyds' shipping insurance complex; but had also his eyes on the heavens; William Joseph Cundell, at No. 3, was a steel merchant; Charles Holland, of No. 7, was a stockbroker; Hugh Pearson Paul, in No. 24, was in ship-insurance; Edward Constantine Tafel of 'Oriel Lodge', No. 26, a Manchester goods shipping merchant, retired when he arrived in the road in 1890. Not untypically, among the first occupier men, he survived his arrival here for only two years. Finally there was James Robert Malcolm, of 'Canisbay', the second or perhaps third generation in a City firm of jute merchants.

Our sources on Franklin Adams derive from the minutes of the Wimbledon Literary and Scientific Society and the obituary notice on him in the Journal of the Royal Astronomical Society. For William Smith Hastings who came to No. 2, aged 61 shortly before the turn of the century, we have had to rely mainly on his will and on the obituary notice on his elder son. It will emerge from the evidence that follows that at least a minority if not the generality of southern businessmen had already been 'gentled'; were not to be thought of as so many ruthless philistines; 'fitted' with the rest of North Wimbledon society as it came quickly into being. Franklin Adams' drawing room, at what he called, 'Grange *Cottage*' and at what everyone after him knew as No. 1, The Grange, accommodated the several Wimbledon Lit. Sci. gatherings he entertained there to talk and show slides about matters of then current astronom- ical interest. None of it can have seemed really incongruous, locally, nationally, or cosmically, *then*; just as in the time of Henry VIII, renaissance man reckoned the world his oyster. Neither was it out of place; merely a reasonable challenge to cosmic forces, in his day and time. He lectured there, that November, on the 1899 Leonids; repeating it on the 11th to the Royal Astronomical Society; and lectured to the Lit. Sci. on many other occasions. He had the freehold on No. 1 at least till 1908; possibly till his death in 1912 when it was acquired by Carlyle, his sitting tenant. *Via* Hampton and Sons, we know Adams spent from while he was convalescing in Cape Town in 1902–1904, trying to sell or let No. 1, having purchased a retirement house near Chislehurst in 1902. He was possibly reluctant to lease out No. 1. He and his wife and five children had been in Chislehurst before, throughout the 1880s; but it was at Wimbledon, on the very edge of our three miles-length of Common, that he began, in 1890, his series of astronomical observations; though his liking for this began, in his youth, in the 1850s. The R.A.S. obituary note said that 'his early education and the engrossing character of his business occupations had not prepared him for such work; but the writer can never forget the enthusiasm with which he described the satisfaction he found in working out the theory and practice of the use of a transit instrument both in the meridian and the prime vertical. He had no instructor. . . and he declared that no one could really learn practical astronomy unless he began in that way.'

So our first businessman had eyes for the stars as much as for his accounts.

William Smith Hastings came to live at 'Parham', No. 1, The Grange, in 1896; remained there till his death in 1923, at the age of 86. We refer to his first son, Percy, in Chapter 8. William's second son, Clement, took up farming in 1916 in Devon; his father stocked the farm for him.   By then Clement must have been 45, and seems to have had three children; the youngest, a second girl, was born in 1902 at 160, Durham Road, about a mile from her paternal grandfather.   There is no sign of Clement having had a previous occupation.   Percy and Clement had an unmarried sister, Juliet.   The source of William's capital has not emerged. His wife, Constance, seems to have had her own.   In his original will, William made 'bequest to my wife of all articles of personal or domestic or household use or ornament belonging to me (except my picture collection) plus a legacy of £200, as she is otherwise provided for under her father's will'.   The rest went to the children and grandchildren.   In a codicil of November 1914, William states 'my son Percy has died. . . I devise my residence 'Parham', plus outbuildings and garden to my wife until she shall die. . . and I bequeath to her my picture collection.'

The third group of the original occupiers comprises the householders with a male head, member of the professional classes.   There were seven such.   Two: Edward John May (No. 2) and Arthur Cawston (No. 18) were architects; two, civil servants.   Sir Thomas Blomefield (No. 6) at the end of his civil service career in 1908 was Assistant Secretary, Finance Department, Board of Trade.   John A.C. Tanner, (No. 10) had a post which was virtually unique.   He was one of the taxing masters to the Supreme Court of Judicature, with an office in Bankruptcy Buildings, Carey Street.   His work was to assess on behalf of the lawyers involved, their settlement costs charged against estates of bankrupts.   Only after the estates had been charged with such costs did the residue become available for distribution between the bankrupts' creditors outside the legal profession.   It is conceivable that Tanner first had cognizance of the auction of the lots that became The Grange through having to assess the costs of the lawyers who had first claim on Mansel's assets, when he had realised them; if so, it has a flavour of almost Dickensian irony.

Of the remaining three, one was an eminent barrister, Henry Warlters Horne of No. 8. He and his wife Harriet had been living at Heston Lodge, 9 Thornton Hill, Wimbledon with three children in 1881.   The house names given by this family seem to have related to places of birth.   Harriet was born at Heston, Middlesex.   The birth of the Horne's eldest child Ethel was registered in the Caterham, Surrey district.   Whyteleafe is a hamlet, 2 miles from Caterham.   Horne named No. 8 'Whyteleafe', and so it has remained ever since.

As well as at the Bar, Horne was active locally, so earned a Wimbledon Borough News obituary on his death at the beginning of April, 1918.   He was a member of the Wimbledon Local Board from 1886 to 1893 and therefore knew Townsend (cf Chapter 4).   Horne took a great interest in the Free Library, serving as a co-opted member of its Committee tor 13 years, and as one of its first chairmen.   Likewise he was an active elected member of the Board of Commons Conservators, in which he was closely associated with another Wimbledon representative, albeit not himself a resident of The Grange, Tyrrell Giles.   Horne retired only in 1912, having been a 'firm upholder of the general policy approved by the majority of his colleagues and confirmed by the result of periodic appeals to the electorate.   In some things he stood apart from what proved to be the prevailing judgement of the community, but he loyally accepted the *res judicata*. Golfers should hold his memory in especial honour, as he was a sturdy champion of their rights and privileges'.

The other two representatives of the professions among the original occupiers were both accountants; Edward Wilks of No. 22 (cf Chapter 10) and George Dixey, of 'Wolstan', No. 19. Dixey ended up with enough West End accounts to have offices as a chartered accountant in Regent's Street; yet had started over forty years before in a modest way in South Wimbledon, in his free time doing accounts of St. Mary's daughter churches there; and even to the end (he died in August 1919) looking, in an honorary capacity, after the accounts, amongst many others, of the local branch of the R.S.P.C.A., and serving as one of the original members of the local Habitation of the Primrose League, as well as in other roles in the Conservative and Unionist cause. After he 'left South Wimbledon to go up the Hill, ' as his obituary in the Wimbledon Borough News put it, 'he keenly interested himself in the work of St. John's Church'. St. John's Road, Wimbledon. Dixey migrated first to Denmark Hill, Wimbledon, (now Avenue), thence to The Grange, as did also Charles Holland. Our point here is a *triple* one. In simple geographical and transport terms, The Grange must have seemed to many professional men, with offices to which they had to commute daily in Westminster or Fleet Street, as eminently suitable.

Many of the men, whether carrying on their business or profession, had already satisfied themselves of the suitability of Wimbledon for their purposes, before moving into the new road, The Grange. No fewer than eight moved into The Grange properties from previous, but less desirable points in Wimbledon; but not to exaggerate; as far as we know six came from non-Wimbledon addresses. The short-distance movers were Cundell, Blomefield, Holland, Horne, Tanner, Dixey, Wilks and Paul. Those probably from further away were Thomson, Franklin Adams, May, Cawston, Tafel and Malcolm.

Socially, The Grange was highly respectable; climatically it could hardly be bettered. Finally, taking up residence here they were *not* putting themselves in some Canberra or Washington but could feel they were able to mix both with a broad stratum of the middle class in their own road, yet also, if they were like Dixey, keep their contacts with that *other* Wimbledon community, across to the south of the railway track, where Dixey's past confreres, from the tone of his obituary, clearly felt he still in part belonged.

7 Primrose Path to Armageddon, 1900 – 1914

Just how regardless of their doom did the little victims of North Wimbledon play? On the evidence available to us, almost totally. We, who matured when Neville Chamberlain went to Munich, can testify that, so soon after the 1914 debacle, we were almost as ignorant. Not all Johnny Ostriches have always their head in air or sand; for some ostriches survive.

In that era, two significant books appeared. The first in the U.S.A., by Thorstein Veblen, in 1899, '*The theory of the leisure class*'. Second, in England, in 1909, from a Liberal M.P., C.F.G. Masterman, '*The condition of England*'.

Masterman began his chapter III, 'The Suburbans':—
'They are easily forgotten: for they do not strive or cry; and for the most part only ask to be left alone'.

And proceeded:—
'he gazes darkly from his pleasant hill villa upon the huge and smoky area of the tumbled tenements which stretches at his feet. . .
It is no despicable life which has thus developed in suburban London. . . that struggle to attain too often means absorption in ignoble standards, and an existence coming more and more to occupy a world of "make believe". When the family is in a position of comfort or of affluence, the houses amply stuccoed or pseudo-Georgian edifices, and the breadwinners in posts of established security in the commercial or financial houses of the city, the atmosphere often becomes stifling and difficult. . . the edifice collapses slowly, and in silence. . . the ingenuity of sedentary guessing competitions, the huge frivolity and ignorance of the world of the music hall and Yellow newspaper. . . perhaps the best that can be hoped for him is the advent of that friendly bullet which will terminate his inglorious life. . . This is the less desirable side of suburban life: a set-off against its many excellences. It probably represents but a passing phase'.

So, too, of course, did Masterman's brilliant journalism. For his percipience was immediately overtaken by the bullets in real lead, and the artillery shells that killed even more stone dead, or shattered their frames and dreams. The Edwardian hookah-Arabian Night proved a mirage. Never again till Hitler's bunker-nightmare in 1945 did things vanish so fast in a puff of smoke.

If for the middle class generally 1900 to 1914 seemed roses all the way, some had doubts. Born in Wimbledon in 1895, in a house on the corner of Lauriston Road and Ridgway, Robert Graves, putting himself in the minority as an adult, some years after the end of the first world war, did not like thinking of Wimbledon.

51

He could have fared worse. In Osbert Sitwell's Scarborough, *'Before the bombardment'*, for example.

North Wimbledonians, before 1900 and 1914, emerged from the cradling crook of the Churches; so important an armour and security to countless earlier generations. Now they stood on their own, within neighbourhood, class and party, with church for special occasions, like last rites. The road, the community and environment helped them adjust and adapt to rapid social change, relatively to 1890—1900. These supports, together with their schools, helped them as social mechanisms along with the family, to survive, resist, and achieve.

Our road microcosm was changing on the periphery. Three of the women original occupiers gone; Mrs Beattie, Mrs Blake, Miss Harkness. Two new widows emerged in their place, albeit in different houses, Nos. 22 (Mrs Elizabeth Allen), and 26, where Mrs Jessie Tafel had lost her husband in 1904. However, in 1905, her brother, Sir Francis Henry Evans, M.P., Director of the Thames and Mersey Marine Insurance Company, and partner in the Union Castle Steamship Company, bought the Murray Estate frontage plot, as additional garden for No. 26. Widow Gribble died in 1894. Her eldest, Marian (aged 59) in 1897. The remaining daughters lived on in No. 5. There were also still the Misses Cox (No. 11), the Widows Lee (Nos. 9 and 12) and Miss Bazalgette, 'Grange Lodge'. The number of merchants/businessmen, seven, remained as before, although again there were peripheral changes. Robert Templar Thomson retired from his shipping business, and his 'Grangemuir' residence, to Edenbridge, Kent, in 1909. 'Grangemuir' saw the marriage of his daughter, Helena, in 1898 to a 'gentleman from Essex', and of his stockbroker son, Hugh in 1904 to 'the daughter of a deceased gentleman'. 'Grangemuir' was bought *via* Hampton and Sons by James Parkes, another businessman. Franklin Adams' departure from No. 1 had about it something of the style of disappearance of Lewis Carroll's Cheshire cat. He leased it from October, 1905 to E.S. Spicer, stationer (we assume of the type who may well have preceded the build-up of the W.H. Smith chain).

Alexander Lang, a relative of Archbishop Cosmo Lang, and general manager of the London branch of the Bank of Montreal until about the time he came to The Grange, presumably on his retirement, became lessee to Widow Cawston of No. 18 in 1910, till at least September 1916.

John Archibald Hughes, the first owner of the new (1908) 'Little House' at No. 4, who had it until 1924, was a young businessman of 33 when he first came, married to Kathleen Emma, with one daughter, Joan Audrey, who later married a Parkin of Torquay. Hughes was a partner in the printery of Mitchell, Hughes & Clarke, of Milford Lane, off the Strand. He expired in Folkestone in December 1959, aged 84, and left effects of £25,403.

The main change in 1900—1914 was among the professional class men. John Curzon Ingle, a conveyancing solicitor, was established at No. 10, following the departure of Tanner. Frank Giles, a retired Indian civil service official, who immediately became active in the Wimbledon Literary and Scientific Society, bought No. 24. Doctor John

A. Hayward, a general practitioner, who was even more active over a long period in the Literary and Scientific Society, and who was recalled by several of our sources of oral evidence, bought and used No. 23 both as a residence and surgery. Three men on retirement from the Army, Colonel John Winn (No. 8); Sir Sydney James O'Bryan Hoare Bt. (No. 16), from 1906 till 1917 as leaseholder, then till 1922 as freeholder; and Major James Burrington Bull (No. 17) which he named 'Abingdon' from 1900 until his death in 1905. Civil servants/ex-civil servants were thus reinforced. Medicine, as well as law, came to be represented; and ex-Army officers put in a strong appearance.

We cannot do better than *estimate* the changing numbers of children and servants, by ages, sex, and types; we specify, presently. Most male householders were married; one or two may have been widowers or bachelors. The children of each household tend to be unknown and anonymous, except in so far as we have tracked them down in the 1881 Census at previous addresses, or in the baptismal or marriage registers of the Wimbledon Parish Church or in some parents' wills. Some of the occupiers, both in the last decade of the nineteenth century, and in the period analysed in this chapter, *did* have children, in some instances of pre-school or higher education age; in others, like the Gribbles, grown and mature. Some, like Hastings, had grown-away offspring, presumably in some instances frequent, in others, infrequent visitors, some of them doubtless bringing *their* children to see the grandparents on occasions. Most of the original husbands and wives brought children with them to The Grange. Some were quite small, others a little older, but it follows that for the original occupiers generally, by 25 years later children had grown up and gone away, some to get married. We have found eleven marriages between 1898 and 1900 of 'children' still living in the road. These occurred in the families of Thomson ('Grangemuir'), Blomefield (No. 6), Jackson (No. 15), Dixey (No. 19), Malcolm ('Canisbay'), and also between a Holland (No. 7) son and a Horne (No. 8) daughter.

Of the newcomers to the road between 1900 and 1914, Dr. Hayward certainly had Lingfield Road, Wimbledon, from which they came. The road at that stage already displayed an impression of an ageing if not aged population especially when the widows are also taken into account. Our guess is that often the youngest people in each property may have been the newest maidservants; the *only* real youngsters being the occasional visiting grandchildren. The youngest creatures about the place may have been the horses, which never seem to be mentioned, but which we have evidence to show were present; and pets, which we feel certain there must have been, but which are *never* mentioned in evidence that has come down to us, except by the Stilemans.

The Stilemans, at No. 8, were always a family with preceding and following generations of children and grandchildren in succession to their ancestor, Colonel Winn, who came to No. 8 in 1908.

Regarding the servants, as we have said, we know even less. They await recognition when the census enumerators' books are opened a century after they were compiled. We know they must have existed, from householders' wills, and as occupiers of the enormous numbers of rooms intended for their use. We have hard facts about one thing — their marriages. Between 1900 and 1914 five spinsters (housemaids, lady's maids or cooks) married from The Grange addresses. All married bachelors, all living in North Wimbledon. A piano tuner, a chauffeur, and a plasterer were among the spouses. The coachman in our house, No. 7, also married, apparently to a girl who worked for Mr. Standen, the baker, as her address was 9 High Street, Wimbledon (still, at the moment of finalising the text of this book, a baker's, Gravestocks). None of these servants came from the spinsters' and widows' households. The mistresses of the female domestic servants who married were the wives of male heads of household. Of these gentry wives, we know least of all; *nothing*.

8 *1914 to 1939, Roll of Honour, and After*

It has been argued that a significant part of British social dynamics in the earlier part of the hundred years, 1884 to 1984, covered by our study, was that the sons of the most successful entrepreneurs were diverted into a non-productive imperial ruling class.

We can find examples from our microcosm at once to support, and to question this. In Chapter 4 we explained the role of John Townsend. Two of his in no way to be written off as 'non-productive' grandsons were John Hamilton Boag, doctor of medicine, and Sir George Townsend Boag, born 1884. George was the eldest son of Townsend's daughter Frances Sophia and the Reverend George Boag, Vicar of Winster, Westmoreland, educated, Westminster School and Trinity College, Cambridge. He entered the Indian Civil Service in 1907, and ended his official career in 1942 as Adviser to the Governor of Madras. Whereas one of the two sons of the wholesale provision merchant owner of 'Grange Lodge' in the 1920s, is said after attending King's College School, which moved from the Strand to Wimbledon Common Southside in 1897–98, to have become a milk-roundsman.

Social determination, as tested by our road-sample, was not simplistic. The imprinting, road-and families-and-successor-families character formation, allowing for deviations from the norms, were far more insinuating and complex; the role of school and higher education far less marked; reactions to national and international developments much more significant.

Before we present our analysis of what happened to The Grange and those who lived or came to live, and grow, in it *between the start of the two world wars*, we should refer to the creation, between 1905 and 1914, of the next road to The Grange on its west, Murray Road. For the earlier history of Murray Road, see Appendix IV. Inevitably, with the *completion* of the building of its *pre*-decessor, Lingfield Road, simultaneously with the building of The Grange from 1889 over the next decade, and *then* with the development of Murray Road, on the *other* side of The Grange, broadly speaking, ten years later, The Grange became, for those who immigrated into it, the equivalent of *the filling in the sandwich*. That situation, as much as the restrictive covenants and nature of the original inhabitants, affected the whole socio-psychology of its residents. We remarked, in Chapter 5, that several owners of properties on land on the *western* side of The Grange (Nos. 23, 24 & 26), in face of the proposed development of Murray Road, bought back-land through to the new Murray Road for preservation as garden or open space.

The epoch when the townscape of residents in The Grange really changed straddled the years immediately before the first world war until even after the end of the second. For albeit the decisions to develop Murray Road in particular ways, were taken in 1905–06, the *actual construction of properties in Murray Road*, which spread south across the Ridgway to a length equal to what it stretched north to Southside, *occurred only over several years starting in about 1908.* In the latter year, ten properties, all but three only defined by house *name*, were occupied in the northern section of the road. Three years later, there were ten more, all defined by house *name*, in this section, and another seven in the southern section, in addition to the six occupied in 1908. We shall be mentioning No. 54, Murray Road, 'Grange Close' which was built in 1923, in relation to No. 7, The Grange, in Chapter 11.

From this brief diversion we now revert to analysis of our microcosm, The Grange, Wimbledon. The overall population of the borough of Wimbledon had, by 1914, grown to about the same size as it has now, in relation to the vast 'over there' of the first world war.

The title of this chapter deliberately harks back to the official version, that was printed and may still be inspected in the Wimbledon Public Reference Library collection of local history materials, *'Roll of Honour'*. That was how that war was presented both during and after it, by 'the authorities'; and, we suspect, to some extent that version and presentation was for long and at large accepted as the most faithful account that could be assembled.

The Wimbledon Borough News editorial, in its second issue after the outbreak of the first world war, adopted the official line with patent relief. The first issue following the outbreak of hostilities, had sat on the fence, pointing to the old alliance between France and Russia, alleging that French investments in Russia were a major factor behind it, claiming it would be better to remember this than go blinkered into war as France's ally. By the second issue, doubts had been resolved, and it was full of the answer to the call to the colours.

By its issue of 5th September, 1914, life and death, were straightforward for the Wimbledon Borough News. It had its first story of a local war hero – Charles Stewart Holland, the eldest son of the then owner of our own house, No. 7 [cf. Chapter 11]. People, however, were 'cussèd'. Scandal of scandals – a meeting for recruitment purposes summoned at the Lecture Hall in the Ridgway, unlike the full house meetings in South Wimbledon, attracted an attendance of only 37. This produced a story-line that the meeting organisers closed the meeting since insufficient North Wimbledonians had turned up to make it worth while for stirring addresses to be delivered; so was this what North Wimbledonians thought about war service? Next week a Wimbledon Common resident felt constrained to report his own roll call. All West Side men between the ages of 19 and 35 had enlisted. The sun was in its heaven again.

For the story of the first local war hero, it is implicit that his parents had supplied obituary material to the Wimbledon Borough News. Thereafter, deaths of Wimbledon resident soldiers ceased to be news. They were *déja vu.*

By coincidence, the second army officer to die in that war, on 2nd September, 1914, just a week after the Hollands' first-born son, was the first-born of William Smith

Hastings, of No. 2, The Grange. Percy Hastings' home address was 4, Longfield Terrace, North Circular Road, Dublin. He was of the same rank as the Hollands' major; in the Royal West Kent Regiment; as mentioned in Chapter 6 died at Bethancourt; left a widow and two children, for whom William Smith Hastings sought to provide under codicils to his original will.

The third was a naval officer, Commander Thomas Wilmot Peregrine Blomefield who died of war wounds in 1915. The eldest son of Sir Thomas Blomefield, he had spent his early manhood at No. 6, The Grange.

The *fourth* army officer from The Grange *survived*. This was Colonel Charles James Dixey who like his father, George, was a chartered accountant. We find Charles James between his father's death in August, 1919, getting Hampton and Sons to value 'Wolstan', No. 19, for probate, giving instructions to sell it for 4,000 guineas; succeeding, in October, 1919, in selling it for 4,000 pounds. In August, 1919, he instructed Hampton and Sons to sell the furniture. We hear no more of him, any more than of the other survivors.

The participation of The Grange in that war applied more to that of such few men-servants as there were, and of some of the women indoor-servants. Part, further, to the temporary occupation of some of the rooms in the houses in the road. Part, finally, to producing or assembling and organising 'comforts for the troops'. As regards crops, the 'Roll' records that by 1918 there were 20 tons of seed potatoes produced from Wimbledon's 1,205 shareholders' allotment plots, redistributed by the Wimbledon Home Produce Society. The Belgian refugees played the most important (37 out of 50) role, physically, in starting off the allotments, with Richardson Evans 'as indefatigable in helping the refugees', of whom there were 473 in Wimbledon. The rest is un-statisticated.

There was a 'non-news-worthy' silence accorded by The Grange, and by other road-communities, to deaths of local soldiers after August, 1914. They seem to have been treated as a matter of family grief simply, *plus* eventual ascription of public debt in some roll of honour. We assess this by comparing length of public news column inches after the death of the first such, and space taken in primary sources like William Hastings' codicils to his will. This, we take to be a significant valuation; for we had expected *that* war even if not at its beginning, to have come to be felt as a negation or at least a threat to all the 1890 to 1914 stabilities and continuances represented as aspirations by the road and homes, supported by their sub-structure of services. Yet no letters, diaries, or other written and explicit evidence have emerged. It is reminis-cent of Vigny's characterisation of stoicism as pictured by the end of the wolf, in his poem *'Le Loup':– 'mourir en silence'.*

We must now turn to the period between the wars, from 1919 to 1939.

This is the first time with which we have to deal where we have been able to adduce and assess oral evidence. We took this from Miss Hazel Jackson (No.18); Mrs. Kitty Porter ('Grange Lodge'); Mrs. Evelyn Stileman (No. 8); and Robert and Dorothy

Watts ('Grangemuir'). 'Grange Lodge' and 'Grangemuir' will both figure in Chapter 11. So we shall reserve further comment on them till then. But we can say here what oral evidence yielded as to the road between the wars generally, and regarding some of the 'characters' whence derived *part* of *its* nature. Generally, the inter-war years are even less evidenced as regards our microcosm, in documentary, drawing, and visual terms, than were the previous thirty years.

Before introducing the oral evidence element we should depict some of the changing scene of occupiers and their establishments in The Grange *between the wars*, as derived from electoral rolls, directories, and other documentary sources. We present *this first* part of the generalisation at once; the fact that *the pace of change seems to have somewhat quickened*, as compared with that of 1890 to 1914, and even 1914 to 1918.

Second, we note that, because the women in question eventually became so old that they died, as compared with the quarter-century preceding the first world war the proportion of widows and spinsters to the total of occupiers dropped. There were nine widows/spinsters in 1889 to 1900; and for most of the period after Edward Constantine Tafel (No. 26) died, in 1904, eight, from 1900 to 1914. When the spinster and widow pair in 'Grange Lodge' [see Chapter 11] and the two Lees in Nos. 9 and 12, all died in 1920–1922, and Beatrice the last of the Gribble spinster daughters, at No. 5, in 1926, the widow/spinster group, till 1931, fell to five. With the death of Mrs. Jessie Tafel (No. 26) in 1931, it became four.

Third, the merchants/businessmen up to 1900 were six, seven from 1900 to 1914, eight till 1924, until J.A. Hughes left No. 4. Thereafter their number fell to four.

For our *fourth* point of analysis of the inter-war occupational/sex change; the group whose number increased most markedly comprised the occupiers whose employment was in one or other of the professions. This increased to ten in all in the inter-war years; whereas it had been eight from 1900 to 1924; and seven from 1889 to 1900. Within this expanding group of the professionals, the most significant and unexpected increase, given that church communicants were declining in numbers steadily through this period, was the *Anglican clergy*. No less than four such (although two of them were from the same house), out of the ten. The number of *doctors* doubled to two. The number of *Army/ex-army commissioned officers* fell again to one from its high-point of three in the immediately preceding period. Civil servants/ex-civil servants disappeared altogether for that period, having been two between 1900 and 1914, and in the years up to 1900 also. Another accountant, Sir William McLintock, came, on this occasion to 'Grangemuir', for a time. There had been two before (George Dixey at No. 19 and Edward Wilks at No. 22). Most nearly constant in numbers, though changed in respect of parts of the profession represented, were the members of the legal profession (three between the wars, including a judge, (Parfitt, at No. 17), two from 1900 to 1914; one amongst the original occupiers, but together with Tanner, the civil servant with legal connexions) we should perhaps say two for 1889 to 1900 also. Oral evidence is notoriously partial. Objects selected for mention by sources are, inevitably, those that most attract as subjects of comment or recollection. Even then, the more immediately proximate they were, the likelier to be noticed; or the

58

odder/more eccentric.   Noteworthy however, the objects selected straddle the whole spectrum of occupiers analysed by sex and occupational grouping.

We suspect it is best to present the angle afforded by oral evidence simultaneously with that supplied by evidence from non-oral evidential sources.   This is what we shall try to do next.

The picture over the whole canvas from social-historical sources, in the progress of the road and the society it subserved as environmental base presents the first world war, for The Grange, as *a hiccup*.

That experienced, city life for both the victors and the vanquished in that war, was a mixture; a seeing out of time for the elders — as we shall find in Chapter 11; and an ushering in of time for the younger survivors.   Life became, for immature adults, more frenetic.   That psycho-pathological over-reaction lasted through the 1920s.   As to the following, so-called, depression, The Grange folk, like the people of south-east England generally, found conditions deriving from the depression to be to their economic *ad*vantage.   We shall be examining in Chapter 11 the one instance where depression hit slightly harder among the occupiers in the road.

Throughout the second decade of the inter-war years, those whom one might have expected to *say something*, remained, in so far as we have been able to trace the record, most curiously and ingloriously *mute*.   What were these additional clergy *for*, e.g., but to make some kind of social comment on what the 'thirties meant, after the 'Journey's End' of 1914 to 1918?   They *may* have tried to say *something*, in their sermons, whether in the Guards' Chapel (the Reverend Williams of No. 16), or in the Mitcham/Raynes Park churches or the College chapels at Cambridge, where they were, father and sons, attached at times (the Sheldons of No. 7).   But *nothing* has come down to us to show that they did so.   On the holier than them principle, it behoves us to recall that we, students in those years, marched hardly a step, got on with trying to get the best degrees we could and enjoy our student life;   were not forever using our privileged point for *'mieux resauter'* to convey to others what life was like for the many relatively less-privileged.   The Reverends Ernest A.K.Long, of No. 6, Sheldons, from No. 7, and Williams, from No. 16, seem to have been no better but also no worse social performers than ourselves, their fairly considerable juniors in years, but one would have hoped less junior in attitudes.   All we can say is that it looks as though they were probably a few points more conformist to their immediately surrounding society and environment than we.

The Reverend Frederick James Williams, M.A. appears in Kelly's Directories from 1903 successively at 3 Lauriston Road, 30 Murray Road, other houses in the area and then at No. 16 The Grange from 1921–1938.   The story as recounted by Robin and Dorothy Watts of 'Glangemuir', who were children at the time, was that the Reverend Frederick became a chaplain to the Guards, and took Dorothy and her elder half-sister and their young friend, the daughter of Professor V.H. Blackman of Berkeley Place, Wimbledon, to the service at the Guards' chapel one Sunday.   'He went later as chaplain to a stately home.   His wife, 'old' Mrs. Williams, was a mystery figure in a long black old-fashioned dress, a recluse at times. We were intrigued because this did not tie up with the glamour of the invitations she gave to our family to accompany her with special tickets to the Aldershot and Greenwich Tattoos, and even to the Royal Box at Greenwich.'

Crockford's in fact reveals that the Reverend Frederick was chaplain from 1903—26 during the summer six months at Holy Trinity, Lamington, Lanarkshire, a private chapel, presumably Lord Lamington's. From October to March he was a chaplain at Cannes, France until the 1914 war. Thereafter he was at a Glasgow Mission Chapel until 1938. He appears therefore, to have used No. 16 as a *pied-a-terre*, although his wife, Mary Ann, lived there continuously until her death in December 1937. While his parents had No. 16 their son Cyril Robert, born 1895, was a civil engineer in the Sudan Railways, from 1941 as General Manager.

We shall say what we have found out about the Sheldons of No. 7 in Chapter 11.

We now try to distil from our several sources of oral evidence, and documentary material for the period, our impression of the 1920s in The Grange.

For the Stilemans in 'Whyteleafe', No. 8, it was first the Langs, at No. 18 from 1910 to at least 1916, then the Jacksons, at No. 18 from about 1927 to 1944, and not to be confused with the earlier Jacksons at No. 15. The second world war dispersed the family whom the Stilemans spoke of as "the Opposites'. Perhaps they may have been so in *more* than just the sense of No. 18 being exactly on the opposite side from No. 8. The Stilemans were Army, and also Emmanuel Church. We are not clear when the Stilemans ceased to use their main garden for tennis, adapting it instead for croquet, as it is now. But they told us that from way back between the wars, family and friends would assemble there for group outings by bicycle to Barnes Bridge to such sporting occasions as the Boat Race. So, too, Hazel Jackson told us the young Jacksons at No. 18, who had three cars between them, would meet up with their friends for trips to horse race meetings. The Jacksons had been formerly at Gatwick; the young Jacksons' grandfather had the 'crack coaching team of the world'. Their grandmother, Lady Talbot Constable, had lived on with them in No. 18, The Grange. The Jackson's father, who died in the first world war, and a brother of Hazel's, were both in the regular Army. During that war the Jacksons moved from Gatwick to Leighton Buzzard, where they had General Joffre as a visitor. There were two paddocks in the grounds. Hazel would never ride a hired horse in Wimbledon with reins on. They came, presumably, to some earlier address in Wimbledon, for Hazel was at Wimbledon High School for girls 'at the time of the fire' — which occurred in 1917. The Jacksons used their garden as the Stilemans did theirs. Even if they were late, coming back from a theatre, 'they put their cars in the garage next to Hampton and Sons in the High Street; for '*it just was not done*, then, to leave cars parked in the road.'

Both the Stilemans and Hazel Jackson had their pets, and pests. The Jacksons had two spaniels, a Great Dane, and a cat. David Stileman recalled that Dr. John Nairn Dobbie of No. 9 had two red setters. The combined team went up and down The

Grange, with Dr. Dobbie behind at a 'great lick like Ben Hur in the chariot race'.

As to what it was like, living in The Grange between the wars, 'It was lovely – no noise, as in Denmark Road now' (Hazel Jackson); 'It was gorgeous if you came from the right side of the tracks' (Dorothy Watts).

The 1920s were marked by the deaths of several *longstanding* residents of the road; William Hastings (No. 2), Charles de L'Hoste Holland (No. 7), Colonel John and Mrs. Winn (No. 8), Sir Sydney Hoare (No. 16), and George Dixey (No. 19). Amongst the widows and spinsters, there also died the last three Misses Gribble (No. 5), Mrs. Elizabeth Lee (No. 9), Mrs. Amy Lee (No. 12), Miss Tissie Balzagetter (Grange Lodge), and Mrs. Jessie Tafel (No. 26). These seven women had accumulated between them *211* years of residence in the road.

We have written of these men and women in greater or lesser detail, except perhaps for the two Mrs. Lee. Of Mrs. Elizabeth ('Eversley') Lee's late husband, we have found nothing; except that, from her will, we gather the couple had one son and a daughter. Both offspring died before their mother, but left spouses and children, some of whom benefited under Mrs. Lee ('Eversley')'s will, as did also her 'friend and companion' Elizabeth Richardson, to the tune of £1000. She also names her cook, parlourmaid and lady's maid. Of Mrs. Amy ('Laughton') Lee's husband, James Frankham Lee, we unearthed more. He had been a solicitor with a London practice. The couple lived in Park Lane until his death in 1890. Almost immediately, Amy moved to the newly built house, No. 12, The Grange, remaining there until her death nearly 30 years later, aged 82. From James' and Amy's wills, we deduce that they had no children, and that the trustees were all connected with James Lee's brothers. So Amy recognised the services of *her* companion, Kate Wilkinson, handsomely, left her an income for life, most of the drawing room furniture including 'my what-not and all the articles I usually keep on it', and also Kate's bedroom furniture, with the inexplicable exception of her iron bedstead. One wonders, without any answer appearing, whether the two Mrs Lee were related by marriage, whether they were friends during the twenty five years they and their companions spent as near neighbours.

The death also occurred, in May, 1926, of Judge James John Parfitt, K.C. who was the most eminent occupier of No. 17, albeit he only lived there for six years (1920 to 1926). His widow, Elizabeth, owned it up to her death in 1949. She seems to have ceased to occupy it at the outbreak of the second world war. Judge Parfitt came to The Grange after two years at Harrogate, when judge on the Leeds Circuit. Prior to that he and his wife lived for many years in The Drive, Wimbledon. They had no children. He is said to have had all the attributes of a good judge, including a retentive memory and 'a sense of humour which often convulsed the court'. Although his legal work occupied most of his house in later life, (he was earlier a county cricketer), he found time to respond to Wimbledon charitable appeals including those connected with the Catholic Church of the Sacred Heart, Edge Hill, Wimbledon, of which he was a prominent member.

Marriages of householders' family were few, only three at any rate at St. Mary's

Wimbledon parish church. In 1915, Hannah, aged 27, daughter of Alexander Lang, C.M.G., of No. 18; and in 1926, Madeleine, aged 25, daughter of Charles A. Ganthony of No. 24. It was the third that was most important for the road viz:- on 18th May, 1917, Evelyn Mary Winn, aged 21, daughter of Colonel John Winn, of 'Whyteleafe' (No. 8) married Arthur Madryll Cleare Stileman, a lieutenant in the Royal Navy, son of Arthur William Stileman, solicitor, of Sunnyside House, Wimbledon. The wedding reception, with tents, was held on the north lawns of 'Whyteleafe'. So was that of her grandson, some sixty years later.

Maidservants in The Grange continued to get married. Five were wed in 1914—1916, from Nos. 18 (two), 11, 1, and 'Canisbay'. A further four between 1923 and 1930, from Nos. 19 (two), 'Grange Lodge', and 18, again. Some of the bridegrooms in the first group had coach-house connections, in the second group, with chauffeuring.

Finally, we asked ourselves the question, how did the depression years from the time of the Wall Street crash of 1929 affect residents of The Grange? And we found the answer, apart from one instance that belongs to and will be dealt with in Chapter 11, to be:— *not in the slightest.*

9 1939–1966

The Grange found itself in limbo during the second world war. The road was not in the direct firing line as were many parts of Greater London. For anyone who came to Wimbledon from the docks, or the East End generally, even for those who still commuted daily into the City, our road as a place to return to must have seemed a haven of heavenly peace. Yet nobody in the road felt really secure. Some of The Grange inhabitants were posted elsewhere. Some moved elsewhere. Some died. Some stayed. Hazel Jackson of No. 18 (nursing) and Margaret Roney of No. 26 (ambulance fleet organisation) were conspicuous for their war work.

The 'incidents' were, of course, a relatively small feature. It was the general grimness of those years, a grimness which extended, pall-like across the rest of the 1940s, well into the 1950s, which took so long to dislodge. In such contrast, according to the oral evidence adduced in the last chapter, with life for those lucky enough to live in the road between the wars, it inevitably helped create changes in the nature of the road. These were to prove lasting. So we should classify and analyse them now.

First, virtually the whole southwest quarter of properties in the road have to look back on the second world war as a watershed in the history of their use. As mentioned in Chapter 5, 'Grange Lodge' was to be demolished. Nos. 15, 16, 17, and 18, were never again to be one-family houses. With No. 18, at the end of the period covered by this chapter, there was a protracted struggle about the nature of the future development of the property. That is dealt with at the end of Chapter 10. Change also stemmed from 1939–45 for many properties in the other three-quarters of the road; though not as radically and dramatically as with the southwest quarter. The crunch struggle came over No. 22 in 1965 to 1966. We shall deal with that in depth in Chapter 10.

Second, while much the same order of frequency of change of occupiers as before 1914 was maintained between the wars the order was not at such a rate as to inhibit natural development of consciousness of community (with 'characters' as one feature of community). But by the end of the second world war, of the original properties *only three or four remained unchanged.* As well as the wholesale changes in personnel and form of tenure effected by the second world war, that war was also a watershed for the emergence of a new age-distribution pyramid, with occupations to match. When the road began in the 1890s, the occupiers included a high proportion of ageing widows and spinsters. Yet every other household matched that by exhibiting a number of pre-or school age children. The bars at the former nursery windows are a physical reminder of the latter. In the inter-war years, there were still some younger children about; but in so far as there were children, they tended to be teen-agers. Since 1945, the proportion of properties with young children has dropped as compared with 80 or 90 years ago. Part effect, part cause; some properties have become flats in place of family-*houses.* The proportion with adolescents has diminished progressively.   That occupied by widows/spinsters in 1939 to 1966 again rose to eight (and since 1966 has remained at six).

By 1966 the merchants/businessmen had fallen to three.   The number of professional class occupiers continued to rise, the clergy dropping out again during the second world war, but other classifications taking their, and others' places.   Following the earlier example of the physically handicapped but artistically gifted John Davy son of Dr Hayward of No. 23 there were some even more creatively so (e.g. Robert Medley, at No. 6, first of the visual arts representatives).

'Canisbay' went into multi-occupation, particularly favoured by theatre people.   One property, 'Grange Lodge', ran the full gamut through A.R.P. post, *via* use as a hotel, into demolition and reconstruction, with name preserved, as a low-rise block of twelve flats — of which more in Chapter 11.

The pack of cards had been violently reshuffled.   That it remained a pack, when so many once packs became just that number of individual playing cards, in the grip of irresistible forces, says much for the degree of cohesion it knew in its first fifty years existence.

We would not ascribe all the changes to the second world war; nor the resistance to change to any one cause; merely point out that the time of maximum change coincided with 1939 to 1945; and thereafter, for our next feature of change is car ownership, cf. the Jacksons of No. 18 in contrast with the convention about parking cars in the road outside the house, that so noticeable feature of the decades since 1945.   The glass of a window of our coach-house, with vertical iron bars inside the windows, bears the tooth-marks still of the horses who were stabled there eighty years ago.   They gnawed round the bars for an alternative taste.   We are glad they did, for it helps to show what a horse-age it was when the road *began*.   Still, only thirty years ago, there was a time when, like Housman, we walked up the road in spring in joy to see the cherry hung with snow.   Now we have to peer between the chassis of success-ive parked cars.   Rates have not gone down, but that aspect of our amenity *has* done.   So; a cross we share with many others who have lived on into our present state of civilisation.

Our evidence bears out the social historians' characterisation of the inter-war years as fecklessly gay.   We trust our interpretation of the 1950s and 60s may be accepted as epitomized by the two technologies, transport and television.   It is really only since 1970 that people have given pause to what these two monsters they have nurtured have begun to do to them and the properties they have acquired and had come to think of as their home.   In the eye of history both may now be seen as consumer 'controlled' anarchical reactions, following the fetterings imposed by the depression, second world war and subsequent restriction-years.   The purchased freedoms afforded by the motor car and television have tended to impel their owners into a private world, where their sight of and acquaintance with their neighbours is more occasional; community, except when that sense and resort for protection is resuscitated in the face of some common external threat, more tenuous.

Earlier in this chapter we referred briefly to the differences in age and occupational distribution in the periods before and after 1939 to 1966. The two civil servant families who came to live in the road, virtually opposite each other, in Nos. 7 and 19, the Harold Copemans and ourselves, each had three generation families in their house, each of the 'economically active' family parts with a single child, a boy, both born in February, 1950. Such circumstances make for ready transmission of tradition, as also tends to occur in a refugee family, like Max and Greta Moldau from Vienna, who bought No. 12 from Widow Coulter in 1942. The house still holds a great deal of Viennese furniture, of characteristic style and charm. But the chief recollection of the Moldaus' son, about furniture, is of how old Mrs. Coulter sold bits of hers to them, piece by piece, bargaining over successive individual items, going to the bank after each transaction to put the proceeds in a safe place. Both father Moldau and son went into business. They were the exceptions among newcomers to the road. From 1939 to 1966, in income group terms the main trend was to a further increase in the proportion whose income is derived from one or another profession. The newer professions came increasingly to be represented also; especially since 1966, particularly those practising the newer technologies, computing, information and television.

10 The German School Affair and Birth of the G.P.A.

No. 22, The Grange, particularly owing to its immediate proximity to the north-east side of the garden of 'Grange Close', was a key property strategically situated for the character of the road as a whole.   Its physical aspect, so changed today following the alterations of 1924, 1931, and 1981, was, for its first 33 years, what it was made by Harmer at the request of Edward Wilks, its first owner-occupier, who had it from 1890 until 1902.   Until 1924, it was not only smaller, and bore a different front elevation from what it presents now; it was on an altogether humbler scale, as modest as any in the bottom quartile of properties in value terms in the road just as those with coach-houses and carriage folk can be reckoned as in the top quartile.

In Wilks' time its scale matched its owner's social position.   Like George Dixey, also hailing from South Wimbledon – and Sir William McClintock, the owner-occupier of the very much grander 'Grangemuir', ten years after Wilks' departure, Wilks was an accountant.   He was one rung up the social mobility ranking from his father, David Wilks (died, 1881, at Coombe Villa, Merton Road, after a lifetime as a commercial traveller, who left net effects of £1,471).   Edward made his will in April, 1917, towards the end of his life, and fifteen years after the end of the eleven he lived in The Grange.   He left £4,857.   In February, 1902 he instructed Hampton and Sons to sell No. 22 for £3,500 lowest, freehold.   Edward Wilks thus made good as compared with his father, David.   But as compared with Dixey and McClintock, he presumably was at the lower end of the accountants' range; indeed, for much of his career, he classed himself not as an accountant, but as a commercial clerk.   Nevertheless, he was elected a member of the Wimbledon Literary and Scientific Society.

Edward Wilks' sister, Clara, lived with him at No. 22, when he was still unmarried.   In 1894, when she was 39, she married a tradesman (albeit a well-respected one, honourably following the craft of his father, John, who had plied it at 61, Wimbledon High Street since the 1850s), Alfred William Siggers, bootmaker.   Clara's husband was one of the first members of the John Evelyn Club; was one of its Executive Committee members; so he must have been more than a simple bootmaker.   But, in that epoch, when everyone but the few who had a horse was a pedestrian, who, save when needing to travel a distance beyond what could be reached on foot, used public transport, bootmaking was a basic and essential trade.

Yet, from these modest origins, No. 22, and its owner-occupiers, were, basically because of the strategic importance of the property, but aided by an exceptional combination of character and philosophies of owners from 1924, to become the focus for two packed years of struggle for the road's character in the mid-1960's.

The significant earlier points in this strange progression were these:–
In June, 1902, following Edward Wilks' instructions, Hampton and Sons sold No. 22

to Mrs Allen, for an undisclosed price. Edward Wilks then went to live at 30, Thornton Hill, Wimbledon, as did a spinster sister, Elizabeth, named after their mother. Edward's spinster sister died there in 1906. Mrs Allen's occupation of No. 22 ceased on her death in 1915. In 1924, another widow, Mrs. Gwendolyn Nunes, came to occupy it with her three sons, along with their servants, and Widow Nunes' hats and dresses. We heard of her outfits from three certain and independent sources of contemporary oral evidence. Her daughter-in-law states that the widow 'left in 1940 when a Spitfire with Polish pilot (she said) went between the house and the three elm trees in the garden!' Reginald and Eric had remained with her. But the main story with which this chapter is concerned developed from her eldest son Humphrey and his wife Flavia, who moved into No. 22 at this point and set up a home-school 'Cygnets' there in 1950. [See Appendix V]

In North Wimbledon, despite the Butler Education Act of 1944, the tradition was that the middle class looked after its own.

As it turned out, the use of No. 22 and the semi-basement of No. 6 for non-purely-residential purposes, viz., educational, for the 'Cygnets', from 1950 to 1962, proved to be a prelude to an attempt to make the road host to a school with a more authoritarian system, the German. The attempt was launched in 1965. That is why we have entitled this chapter as we have done.

The sequence of events was this:— The Nunes sold No. 22 in 1961/2 to a couple who resold it by 1964 to another couple called Sinclair. This latter pair had it for the next two and a half years. For most of 1965—66 Sinclair was engaged in trying to sell the property, with planning permission for the Germans' cultural establishment to use it, with lavatories in the garden, next to Joe Burrell's boundary on the northeast side of the gardens of 'Grange Close', as a school for German children throughout London. After all, the U.S. had been doing this in several parts of London — and continued to do it — throughout the years since the second World War; so why not the West Germans? They were finally well on the way to becoming socially as well as diplomatically rehabilitated; and the claim was made that No. 22 had been used, with the assent of the residents of other properties in the road, as a school, for twelve years. But the proposal aroused the sleeping giant of adjacent residents in the road. On either side of Sinclair there were solicitors of many years experience and considerable standing. In No. 23 was Alan Oliver. With his wife, Rhoda, who had taught history at the Wimbledon High School in Mansel Road for several years before she had a family of her own to bring up, and knew more about education than any of the successive occupiers of No. 22, *and* the Germans, who, at this stage, were in this matter at diplomatic rather than professional level, Oliver took the lead, and the main load. It was he who at an early but crucial stage got an injunction ordered in the High Court. That gave him more time to prepare a draft brief, and, with his neighbours to help initiate an organisation. It was far from clear at this point whether there would not have to be a case at law with high-priced counsel employed. Joe Burrell, in 'Grange Close', backed Oliver. So, doing a *volte-face*, for in the 1950s it was they who had allowed the Nunes to use their front semi-basement in No. 6 for the class overflow, did the Washbourns. Roger Washbourn was a senior official in the British Council.

When Sinclair made his *demarche* in 1965, Roger Washbourn had in mind that in another ten years' time he would be retiring from the Council and the need to commute daily to Davies Street, near the Oxford Street end of Bond Street. He and his wife were keen watchers of wild bird life. Roger wrote the chapter thereon for the booklet that was published, in expert symposium form, to accompany the centenary celebrations of the Wimbledon and Putney Commons Act of 1871. On his retirement following those celebrations, his wife Margaret and he sold No. 6, and moved to rural Norfolk, which of course offered greater variety of wild birds than Wimbledon Common.

Alan Oliver, Joe Burrell, and Roger Washbourn, as a counter to Sinclair and the Germans, (including, we were told at the time, one German family then temporarily residing in The Grange) set up an organisation, duly constituted, of which they were 'Founder-members', the one feature of the constitution to have been rescinded on the reconstitution of the organisation six years later. The name and purpose remain — *The Grange Preservation Association.* Since the date of its reconstitution, all the owner-occupiers in The Grange, including, since it was unitised as a residential property, 'Grangemuir' and its coach-house, have been members, one hundred per cent.

The question of the German School did not, after all, go to Court, apart from the injunction mentioned. Instead, it fell initially for administrative and procedural decision, to the Wimbledon Borough Council, in the last couple of years of that body's life, before it was absorbed into the new London Borough of Merton, established on 1st April, 1965, under the London Government Act, 1963 to reorganise the government of London. The Council especially given the foreign relations aspects of the affair, were only too pleased for Crossman's new (created by the first Harold Wilson administration in 1964) Department of the Environment to adjudicate. The latter remitted it to one of their Inspectors to apply their established procedure of public hearing before the appointed inspector, and subsequent report to the Secretary of State. The Grange Preservation Association made its case at the hearing. The inspector found *for* the case for the proposed school. The Germans had meanwhile taken the measure of the temper of the residents of The Grange; had made, no doubt, discreet inquiries as to possible alternatives. They must have told Sinclair they were no longer in the market for No. 22. Sinclair sold, to a barrister, in 1968; with *no* planning permission for anything except purely residential purposes. The new owner, his wife and their children, remained the owners and principal occupiers until they sold in November, 1983.

The good things to come from the Nunes/Sinclair/German school affair were (a) that the German school did *not* eventuate in the middle of the west side of this basically residential road in what soon afterwards became part of an extended Wimbledon Village Conservation area; and (b) the Grange Preservation Association, once brought into being as part of the community response to that specific threat, has become an established vehicle for a whole variety of Grange Preservation Association purposes. Its most recent major achievement has been the encouragement and backing it has given to the project for 'The Grange, Wimbledon, a centenary portrait'. As far as we know, it is the only road association under whose auspices a centenary portrait of the road it represents has been researched, written and published.   But there has, every year, been something which the association has had to tackle. Just when the 1968–83 owner-occupier of No. 22 moved in, there was the planning proposal by the Constructional Engineering Union, as freeholders — but absentees — following the death of their general secretary, John Stanley, in the previous year, for Cawston's No. 18 to be demolished and replaced by a block of purpose built flats with several garages at the rear.   It took three years really to dispose of that threat, and for the existing house, instead, to be developed by conversion into flats for sale leasehold; and as long, again, for the asking price for each of the converted flats brought, by market forces, to the level at which each was eventually sold.

11 Three Case Studies, 'Grangemuir', 'Grange Lodge', and No. 7

These case studies illustrate how the form and use of the properties concerned was adapted/substituted over the century to comply with changing need and demand. They are indicative although inevitably not comprehensive; are chosen so as to provide, within the perimeter of the road, an appropriate geographical-physical scatter and sample. One is at the southwest terminus; one at the northeast terminus; the third squarely in the middle on the east side, but able to face through to all points of compass. They are:- 'Grange Lodge'; 'Grangemuir'; and No. 7, The Grange.

'Grange Lodge'
Born in controversy, converted in its middle years to public and quasi-public use, demolished before it reached its three-score years and ten; replaced by purpose-built low-rise flats which kept to the original building-area, and retained its maiden name, this property, the reader might feel, had run the gamut. But wait; till we have told how time dealt with the other two.

As to its beginning, we refrained from writing 'born in controversy. . . attended, some say, by some kind of tragedy'. Our evidence on the second point is too slim to make so much of it. What we have, we shall retail.

At the start of June, 1890, the eminent Sir Joseph Bazalgette was checked, by the democratically representative Wimbledon Local Board, according to the sole press organ of the time. For whatever value it may have, there is a story of some possible tragedy that may have prevented a marriage between Miss Theresa Bazalgette, eldest daughter of Sir Joseph, and someone unknown, while the Lodge was being built in 1890. (Source:- oral evidence from Mr. Ronald Burns, resident between the wars at 'Grange Lodge'.) The Wimbledon Borough News published, on 5th May, 1922, a joint obituary of Miss Bazalgette and 99 years old widow, Emily Devas, her aunt, who had been her companion at Grange Lodge since sometime during the war, when air-raids on Broadstairs drove Mrs. Devas back to Wimbledon.

Its conversion in its middle years to public and quasi-public use needs to be referred to next. This followed a few years after its occupation in the 1920s by the Palmers, he a general provision merchant. At the time of Munich its cellars were reinforced with wood propping and during 1939–1945 it was used as an Air Raid Precaution centre. By 1938, the house had become The Grange Lodge Hotel, owned by Mr. and Mrs. Robert Burns, who lived there with their children, together with a number of permanent guests. It remained up to 1959 in some such condition, i.e. quasi-public use, until whoever owned it decided that demolition of the original building (and it *was* original in more than simply the sense of priority in historic time), and its replacement by a low-rise block of twelve flats might prove an investment more appropriate to the new era.

This is the *only* block of purpose-built flats in (or rather on the southwest corner of) the road; planning permission for the change might *not* have been granted had the application been delayed another seven years, i.e. until the Wimbledon Village Conservation Area extension. Whereas many roads in Putney and Wimbledon have exhibited wholesale changeover from villa residences to blocks of flats in the last thirty years, with consequent radical change to their character, the fact that this is *the only block and that on the corner with the Ridgway*, and a spread-out low rise edifice, has ensured that this particular marked variation from the conserved norm of the rest of the road has been *contained* as a precedent, and as to its effects.

In community terms, despite the block now having been there for twenty-three years, because of its differences and separateness, the inhabitants of the block of flats, changing generally more frequently than the population of the remaining villas, have *not*, with marginal exceptions, been accepted or absorbed into The Grange. As we have remarked, the grounds of 'Grange Lodge' retained their amenity, indeed enhanced the degree of amenity to which they had declined in the years when the building was used as a hotel. This was, presumably, the result of a clause in the leases of the flats in the new block, providing for some element of rent to be devoted to maintenance in good order of the grounds of the block. This is another factor in the assessment we have proffered about the property having developed into quasi-public use.

Thus, the *spirit* of the restrictive covenants written in to the deeds of the original houses developed on The Grange estate was, even before the designation of the road as part of the Wimbledon Village Conservation Area extension, to some degree, adopted even in a radical change of user, as in the instance of 'Grange Lodge'. The retention of 'Grange Lodge' for the name of the property, confusing as this may have been to non-residents unaware of its history, was also, in itself, more than purely symbolic of the desire of the developers to represent the property as a continuation of its predecessor on site.

'Grangemuir'
Socio-psychologically, in that its beginning appears in no way to have been attended by any unhappy star as 'Grange Lodge' may have been, 'Grangemuir's' first more than fifty years seem to have been all bathed in a social atmosphere of middle class business/professional men's satisfaction. This despite the owners at the beginning and end of that era, Thomson and Watts (albeit at the end of his career) being involved in an industry that throughout their time was on the brink of the abrupt decline that has occurred since their departure – shipowning. Robert Templar Thomson died in June 1919. Six years before, he moved to a property at Froghole, Edenbridge, Kent which he named 'Little Mariners' – *not* the term that would have been chosen by one disillusioned with his professional past. He left getting on for £52,000,

Wo havc not discovered with what shipping line Thomson may have been connected.

John William Watts had been an industrial chemist, and later road maker, by profession, but had retired early from these occupations just before coming to 'Grangemuir'. Unexpectedly he became involved in shipping. The White Star Line

71

scandal had caused all the members of the board to be removed from office, and shares nose-dived. Private shareholders, of whom John Watts was one, then elected him to join the new board in June 1932, in order to try and salvage something from the wreck. He was appointed chairman of the board in February 1934. The White Star company however had to be compulsorily wound up, by High Court order, in April 1935. It then had a deficit of £11,280,864. Attempts were apparently made to take legal action against the original directors of White Star in respect of irregularities particularly for the year 1929. But W.D. Spens, K.C. advised that no legal action would succeed against former directors. The line's main business had been in carrying passengers to and from North America and Australia. Until the slump led the Treasury to withdraw from the Government's previous intention to subsidise the building of the first of the 'Queen' ships for the transatlantic trade, White Star had been in hopes of landing that finance. In the event, it was Cunard who collected. (1)

Watts was also a director of the Royal Mail Shipping Company and of Shaw, Savill & Albion, and although his health was not good, he was still happy and active enough to see his two youngsters by his second marriage growing up cheerfully in the garden of 'Grangemuir', and up and down the road; to be both a local Councillor, and governor of King's College School and a 'Ruling Councillor of the Primrose League'.

In June 1944, about two years after his death, one of the pinnacles (still missing) of 'Grangemuir' and its leaded lights glass, stained and otherwise were smashed by a flying bomb. The roof and windows were quickly repaired, but the Watts family did not return and the premises were rented to the Wandsworth Gas Company as emergency offices, but they had no cause to use them. Even the John Evelyn Museum, which had a war-years use of the basement, seems to have moved out. We understand that the Museum collection was divided during the war and housed for safe keeping in various Wimbledon cellars.

In 1946, somewhat in the model pattern of 'Grange Lodge', 'Grangemuir' came into quasi-public occupation. First as a children's foster-home, under auspices of the Soldiers, Sailors and Air Forces Association. Then in the 1960s under the new London Borough of Brent, it became a hospice for pre-school-age children. It so remained for nineteen years, with a succession of children's nurses, nine at a time, all about twenty-two years old, who led their charges up and down the road, and around Southside and on to The Green, Wimbledon Common for a couple of excursions each day. It was when Brent, having no further need of it, gave it up, in 1976, that controversy arose about its future. As ventilated through the Wimbledon Borough News, the alternatives were that its quasi-public function be not just continued, but that it might become a probation hostel; or be so converted that in several parts it should revert to its pre-second world war function as private residence. It was the latter that won out. The process of conversion took more than a year. Since 1978/9 there have been three freehold units in the main house, which has been split vertically. Its converted coach-house is a separate freehold property, between the sound end of the gardens at the rear of the three units in the main house (these gardens unhappily divided in three) and the northern boundary of No. 1, The Grange. In contrast to the more numerous residents in the longer-established new flats of the, to us, still new, 'Grange Lodge', the owner-occupiers of the three 'Grangemuir' main house units and 'Grangemuir's' coach-house (now 1A, The Grange) have been accepted into The Grange as part of its community.

No. 7, The Grange
Like man, no property is an island. All the more so, when, as with No. 7, it is in the middle of one side of the road. That despite the original owner's effort, during his thirty-three years of ownership, to achieve a sort of splendid isolation.

Charles Wroughton De l'Hoste Holland, stockbroker, who had been living in Denmark Hill, Wimbledon (now Avenue), bought the land from Peek in 1889 and as described in Chapter 5 had Ernest Newton design the house and extension and coach-house for him and raised his family of three young children in it. In 1891, Holland bought the plot opposite, as far back as the Murray estate boundary; that was a purchase from Harmer, who had bought it at the 1888 auction. In 1905, when the British Land Company bought Miss Murray's 'Wimbledon Lodge', demolished it, and sold off its grounds, Holland bought one plot that might otherwise have been built on, on what became the Murray Road frontage; so as to keep his view clear as far as the west side of Murray Road. That is how it stayed while he lived, and while the children grew to maturity. On his death, No. 7 was sold and a new house 'Grange Close' built on this plot for his widow and daughter.

We should now say what we have learned of Charles Holland, the original occupier, his wife Margaret, their two sons, Charles Stewart, and James Burnes, and their daughter Effie Margaret, and their household. Joe Burrell, in oral evidence, characterised the Holland family as 'establishment; a regular run of the mill Wimbledon family'. Charles, the father, was all his life a city stockbroker, though he and his wife both had army officer background connexions; only revealed in their elder son's obituary. Major Charles Stewart, a regular army officer who had earlier served in India and in the Boer war, was killed at the end of August, 1914, surmisedly at Mons. The Wimbledon Borough News reported Charles Stewart as being grandson of Colonel James Holland, Quartermaster General of the Bombay Army, and a great grandson of Major W.J. Risch of the 79th Queen's Own Cameron Highlanders. Charles Stewart had married in December, 1909, at St. Mary's Wimbledon parish church, Enid, the youngest daughter of the Hornes. In Charles Stewart's youth, the Hornes were the family next door. until 1908, in 'Whyteleafe', No. 8.

James Burnes Holland, the younger son, went into the church [see Appendix VI]. Charles de l'Hoste was admitted to the Stock Exchange list of members in 1875. According to the 1885–86 Stock Exchange List he was in a partnership, *not a limited* partnership, with George Balfour and G.D. Hamillton, of No. 2, Cushion Court, Old Broad Street. The 1913 Stock Exchange List showed him as still at the same City office address, and occupying Stand No. 10 on the Stock Exchange floor.

Charles de l'Hoste, and his wife and daughter remained at No. 7 until his death in 1922. He left £47,518. We shall return to review what happened to No. 7 (the big 7,

73

as it became and remained in Charles Holland's last eighteen years), in two paragraphs time.

As to Charles Holland's household, the servants best help us. When The Grange as a physical-social phenomenon is examined closely, it is found to have five *coach-houses*. *Only* five. So the original occupiers were middle class, but, except for those five, *not carriage-folk*. This may sound a subtle distinction today, when rare is the household in the middle classes, and fairly rare in the working classes, which does not have a car. Indeed, a sizeable proportion of households has *more than one car*. The quality of the cars varies greatly; but London, taking the conurbation as a whole, as also much of Britain, has become a car-owning *democracy*. This helps to measure the big leap forward as between the start of the century of existence of The Grange as a road, and the near hundred years since that it has attained. Of the properties which had coach-houses, three figure in this chapter, 'Grange Lodge', 'Grangemuir', and, in the middle, No. 7. The rooms over the coach-house at No. 7 remained in occupation by married couple servants until 1944.

James and Effie Holland, acting on behalf of their mother Margaret, sold No. 7 to the Reverend James Frederick Sheldon in 1923. He was then Lord President Bishop's Messenger in the Chelmsford Diocese, but was posted to the nearer Diocese of Southwark in 1928. The Watts children recalled him in the 1930s as an old man with a long white beard. His elder son, the Reverend Frederick Howard Sheldon shared the house with his parents. An account of his career and that of his younger brother, the Reverend Leonard Gordon Melville Sheldon is in Appendix VI. Both sons were incumbents at Christ Church, Mitcham at the time of their father's purchase of No. 7. It is likely that James Frederick and his wife evacuated in 1941 to be near Leonard's vicarage in Crowborough. He died in June 1942 aged 79 at the Crest Hotel, Crowborough, leaving effects of £24,349. The old man had made his will only one month before he died, naming his wife Emma Gertrude and his two sons as executors, but bequeathing No. 7 to Frederick Howard, who managed to sell it two years later.

No. 7 never passed into a phase of public or quasi-public use in the senses in which first 'Grange Lodge' and then 'Grangemuir' did. It might be argued that while it was occupied by clergy (James Holland, and then the Sheldons) the house served, although neither as a vicarage or rectory or clergy-house, nonetheless as a base from which its occupiers emerged to render public, and in particular spiritual, service.

Briefly, the sequence was this. The elder Sheldon son, Frederick Howard, in 1944 sold, on the death of his 79-year old father in mid-1942. But who wanted property, even in the suburbs, of the main continuing bombing target, London, at that stage of the war, waged increasingly by missiles, land-based on the occupied North-European coast? A sizeable proportion of the population of the conurbation moved out of it for at least parts of the duration of the war with Germany. Allied Government offices moved into some parts (Eaton Square was full of such). Commercial offices, like the National Mutual Life Association of Australasia Ltd., kept their, even more bombed, City of London address, but also became temporary resident/daily users of e.g. No. 16, The Grange. The chief officer of the Constructional Engineering Union, as we have previously seen, with his Waterloo office bombed out, was rehoused, both as to his office, and as a residence for his family, in No. 18, The Grange from (probably) 1944 until 1959.

As regards No. 7, a risk-taking, entrepreneurial couple, who, we gathered, had performed a similar function elsewhere earlier in the war, bought the property in 1944 from the elder Sheldon son with a view to a quick resale; prepared plans for its conversion into three flats, in the main house, horizontally divided by floors; got a considerable way towards obtaining planning permission from the Wimbledon Borough Council, and building supplies permits to put into effect this change from single family user with resident servants, to three family user, one family per floor.

Frank and Lucy Norman viewed it first as potential purchasers in April, 1945, a month before the end of the war with Germany. They had looked at other places on offer in Wimbledon and Putney, related it to their financial circumstances and the life-style they hoped for, now Frank had retired from the Civil Service in 1944 at 60, and they had returned in January 1945 *via* New York from the West Indies [2].

Apart from the first two years (in Hampstead Garden Suburb), their married life was spent from 1913 to early 1939 (when Frank was sent by the Ministry of Labour as Labour Adviser to Jamaica) in the Wimbledon area, mainly in successive properties in Mansel Road, Lansdowne Road and Thornton Hill. Their son attended King's College School, and their daughter Wimbledon High School for girls. So they had *become* Wimbledonians, had many friends in the district, found it natural to prospect it again on their return to England. And they still wanted a *family*-house, perhaps all the more after five years of living in guest-houses, thousands of miles from their family, in the West Indies [3]. For the rest including their participation in many Wimbledon activities until Frank Norman's death in 1959, and Lucy's in 1967, their obituaries, like the obituaries of other residents in the road, such as John Franklin Adams, should largely suffice [4].

We often visited at weekends previously; but in the second half of 1949, Lucy, who managed the property, let the second floor flat to us. Until our secondment in June, 1952, for two years in Jamaica, we lived there and our son Michael was born in February, 1950. We returned at the end of April, 1954, but moved down to the ground floor flat in which we still remain. The Normans had lived in that for five years when they first bought the house, but moved to the first floor flat in 1950.

It was Frank who invented, about 1955, the name for the house that remains on the front gate:- 'Fralunor'; a foreshortening of their combined christian and surnames. They were familiar characters in the road when they were alive. Lucy was only 5 feet tall but bursting with energy; Frank with 6 feet 6 inches, with a Vandyke beard, with as great a sense of humour and the courtliest of manners. In the same year as the Normans bought No. 7, a Mrs. Berney bought No. 6. She had a niece, Elizabeth Smyth, living with her, and attending The Study school, Wimbldon. We met her in 1981, by then married to Dr. Evelegh, Medical Referee for Wandsworth, and living in St. John's Road, Wimbledon. Mrs. Evelegh told us that when her children were young, in the 1950s, she used sometimes to bring them up The Grange to see where their mother had lived before she was married; and occasionally they would meet Frank Norman. The children referred to him as 'God', because of his appearance. As we remark in the next chapter, sometimes the vision of children is more perceptive. For us, the Normans have remained in spirit as exemplars. During their occupancy, they used No. 7 as a base from which they lived what was essentially a life of public and quasi-public service; for they were too big for it to be simply a family house, and for theirs to be simply a family life.

Footnotes for Chapter 11

[1] 'The Cunard White Star Quadruple-Screw Liner', "Queen Mary", 'Ocean Liners of the past.' Bonanza Books, N. York, 1936 (The Shipbuilder & Marine engine builder), The Shipbuilder Press.

[2] For Frank Norman's autobiography of his official life, please see the bibiography.

[3] Their closest kin by 1945, were their son Howard, his wife, and their first two children both sons, and therefore grandsons of Frank and Lucy. Howard and his family were all then living in Caversham, Reading, where Howard was a surveyor in the regional office of the Ministry of Works; and their daughter Beatrice, and her husband Douglas, the authors of this study, then in a flat in Belgravia. Claire, Howard's daughter, was born during his secondment to New Delhi, in 1949.

[4] Frank Norman, 6th February, 1959; Lucy Norman, 17th March, 1967, both in the Wimbledon Borough News.

12 And So To Now

We explained at the end of Chapter 10 how, at the end of the school affair, the Germans decided to withdraw, and Sinclair was frustrated over selling No. 22 to them, with permission to change its use to a school.   He sold, thereafter, to a family for residential use, in 1968.   Had the German school occurred, this would have revolutionised the character of the road as a whole.   Changes *have* occurred, both at No. 22, and elsewhere in the last fifteen years.   One that all residents felt keenly was when Mr. Berry, the tree-expert in the Parks Dept. of the London Borough of Merton, decided that the top of the glorious plane tree growing in the pavement — that must have been there before 1888 — was afflicted by a disease requiring surgery.   Our plane has recovered now; but all of us were afraid when it was beheaded.   For the trees in our road, whether the plane or the giant holly, or even the elm trunk half in our garden at No. 7, and half at its base, in the pavement, and of course also the flowering trees in the residents' front gardens, are the crowning beauty of The Grange. Cowboys, arrogating the title of 'tree surgeon' used, between eight and ten years ago, before we had grown wisteria and clematis up and over our ten-feet high bare elm stump, to ring our bell.   'We are working elsewhere in this road, or the next', they would lie.   'Would you like us to cut down the old dead tree? If we don't, it will break down the brickwork of your front garden wall'.   When we refused, one of them took it to the point of saying, 'Oh! Why don't you crawl away and die yourself?'

It was from then, finding the trunk had a bole, just child-waist height, the children from No. 11a came to put posy tributes on it, and said they called it their 'Peter Pan' tree.   Through their eyes we saw that the way it leant in towards our rockery, had something about it of the trunk athwart which Peter Pan stands with legs eternally planted, in Kensington Gardens.   Mr. A.P. Whitehead, of Lauriston Cottage, too, had a childhood memory of it.   When his sister and he were little, they had a young Welsh nurse.   She took them for their walk on Sunday afternoon.   Part of the ritual was for them to be brought as far as our tree.   Then she would sit them down on its bole; and make them sing hymns.

The vision of children may be sharper than our own.   We hope we have managed to restore some of its keenness for some of the details of the street where we live.

Changes have occurred, without being revolutionary.   They have been that much more tolerable, because they were gradual and conservative.

To review, with the hindsight of historical perspective, changes in the social complexion of the road's inhabitants over the last fifteen years, is beyond our powers. We cannot, like social anthropologists, leave the society in which we have been living, distance ourselves from it after living in it.   We have not been trained to observe our community in that way.   The census enumerators' books for 1971 and 1981 could serve as a basis for the kind of analysis from which we have endeavoured to picture the changing pattern among occupiers in earlier generations.   Census enumerators are not appointed to deal with the census district in which they live.   Enumerators are enjoined to confidentiality of the districts they are appointed to enumerate. Even had we been professionally capable of analysing the community in which we have been living in these last fifteen years, it would, to our mind, utterly undermine the basis of the confidence that subsists between the community and ourselves.   So we trust it will be understood that this final chapter has to be more general than earlier ones.   We shall however, write what we believe we may, and bring this study to a set of defensible conclusions.

First, The Grange estate has throughout been a middle class development.   Other classes, individuals, male and female, led or subserved the development process, some voluntarily, others involuntarily;   young and old, married, single or widowed. *Middlemen* were involved in the process.   The highly convenient presence and interest of the then Chairman of the Wimbledon Local Board, just around the corner, during the first building and recognition stages, ushered in this new conservative, road; nursed it through its infancy.   The hand of the Wimbledon Borough Council faintly showed, reluctantly requisitioning No. 17, but only in the second world war and its aftermath;   as the source of issue of planning permissions from 1945 onward, forced against its normal nature to have regard to the scarcity of materials available for works involved in conversions during that aftermath;   and, in its self-conceived role, perform-ing the supportive tasks of road cleaning, refuse removal, maintenance of drains and sewers, road and pavement resurfacing.   Finally, in the affair of the German school, the Council acted as channel between contestants and the Ministry responsible.   It went right against the local authority's grain to become an initiator, from being a regulator.   After 1945 it conceded that it might need to perform a more positive, interventionist role;   but the consensus of the dominant conservative and ratepayer-representative group together with the labour group speaking for South Wimbledon was that any positive priorities should be pointed at the relatively poor.   There was a gut-feeling among the councillors that North Wimbledon fok had *always* 'never had it so good';   would look after themselves and their own, whether in education or basic infrastructural services.

That was why, when, in 1971, the John Evelyn Society, following the Wimbledon and Putney Commons Act centenary celebrations, asserted that Victorian North Wimbledon ambience and character were at risk because developers were in process of demolishing parts and replacing them by custom-built blocks of box-flats, first lobbied the *new* local authority, the London Borough of Merton, in favour of adopting a more interventionist attitude to protect and conserve that bastion of the well-heeled, the Council turned them down flat.

The Council had the *legal* powers, following legislation by the Wilson government in the later 1960s, and reinforced by the Heath government at the start of the 1970s, to do what it was asked to do by the John Evelyn (amenity preservation) Society.   It avowed, however, administrative difficulties as warranting its initial refusal to act. Given a local government machine geared to minimal positive intervention, and largely charged to reluctant middle class ratepayers, what the Council said was true from their angle. But this was when the Heath machine, which most North Wimbledonians had voted into office, failed them. Obscurely (to put no brighter point on it) and humiliatingly they found themselves shot down in flames by, of all people, Joe Gormley's coalminers. It was, John Evelyn Society members felt, *just too much* at the same moment to receive such a response from the Council. They enlisted the aid of the Victorian Society, which, in turn, persuaded pursuance of the cause. Then, miracle of miracles, after the trumpets had sounded for the third time round the walls of the Council, the authority capitulated, 95 per cent, to the representations made to it.

It is in no way meant to denigrate the achievement to say that it was, of course, as to 75 per cent, accident.

Time proved to have a forelock to seize, unusually. This, the conservationists grabbed with the name and repute of the Victorian Society, which nationally and culturally proved something that could be conjured with amongst the philistines, *viz.* the councillors on the young London Borough of Merton.

In 1977, only six years after the John Evelyn Society submitted their original survey and recommendations, the Council issued a map showing the 'Original Conservation Area' in orange; and the 'Extended Conservation Area', 150 per cent larger on its own than the 'Original', in pink. The 'Extended' embraced The Grange, Murray, Lingfield Roads, the Parkside and Belvedere estates, and much more. Along with inflation and the high rate of interest, it halted the demolition squad developers in their tracks. This was the high point of conservationism in Wimbledon. Obviously, the Grange Preservation Association, as also the whole Wimbledon Union of Residents' Associations, supported the conservationist cause.

Simultaneously with the affair of No. 18 in 1968, and on its own initiative, the Council began a series of public consultations on its 'Borough Plan' proposals. Documents on geographical sections of this were tabled for discussion. Its proposal document for North and West Wimbledon used a line drawing of the twin towers and pinnacles of 'Grangemuir' and 'Canisbay' at the Southside/The Grange corners as the design for its front cover. The Council had no real problem in reaching general consensus with the public over its proposals for North Wimbledon. Only over its proposals for a new town centre in Wimbledon has it become involved in dispute with residents. That story would be out of place in this book. But it is not irrelevant, in that connexion, to recall that The Grange, during its century of existence, while adapting to the inevitable change of circumstances, has managed remarkably to retain its character, by a mixture of action by private owners and the community acting generally in their support.

No two roads are the same; it is not suggested that any other road should necessarily wish to be like The Grange; nor to use measures like those The Grange has employed. Emulation may be the highest form of praise. This study may give suburban conservationists points to think about; may suggest to urban historians other possible ways of tracing urban history. For our part, we feel considerably in their debt for the ideas they have given us. If this in any way repays that, we shall be the more pleased.

For ourselves, we suspect the time may have come for us, like Prospero, to drown some of our books, papers, and what D.H. Lawrence in one of his stories called 'Things'; to seek, like Charles de l'Hoste Holland here, eighty years ago, that bauble privacy. Not by his method, of buying land through from the front of our house to the east side of Murray Road; but by moving back towards Lingfield Road into our coach-house cottage, the conversion of which we completed two years ago.

Plates

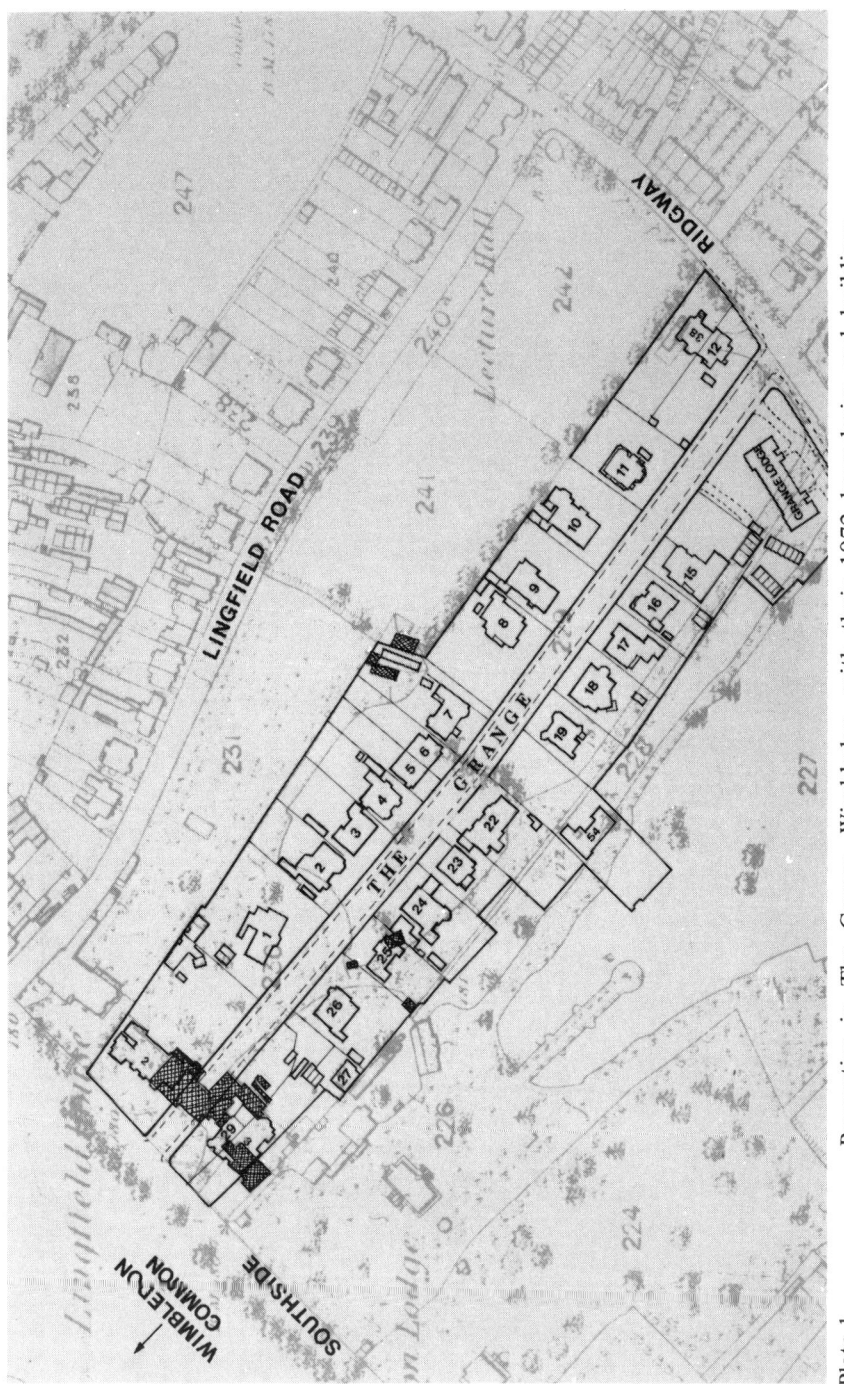

Plate 1   Properties in The Grange, Wimbledon, with their 1972 boundaries and buildings outlined, superimposed on Ordnance Survey map of 1865, showing development of the Grange Estate, Wimbledon.

Plate 2

The original house (here called Sir Francis Burdett's, later called 'The Grange')
Back view
Engraving by Thomas Girtin. c. 1800

84

SIR FRANCIS BURDETT'S HOUSE, WIMBLEDON.

The original house (here called Sir Francis Burdett's, later called 'The Grange')
Front view

Engraver unknown, c. 1800

Plate 3

85

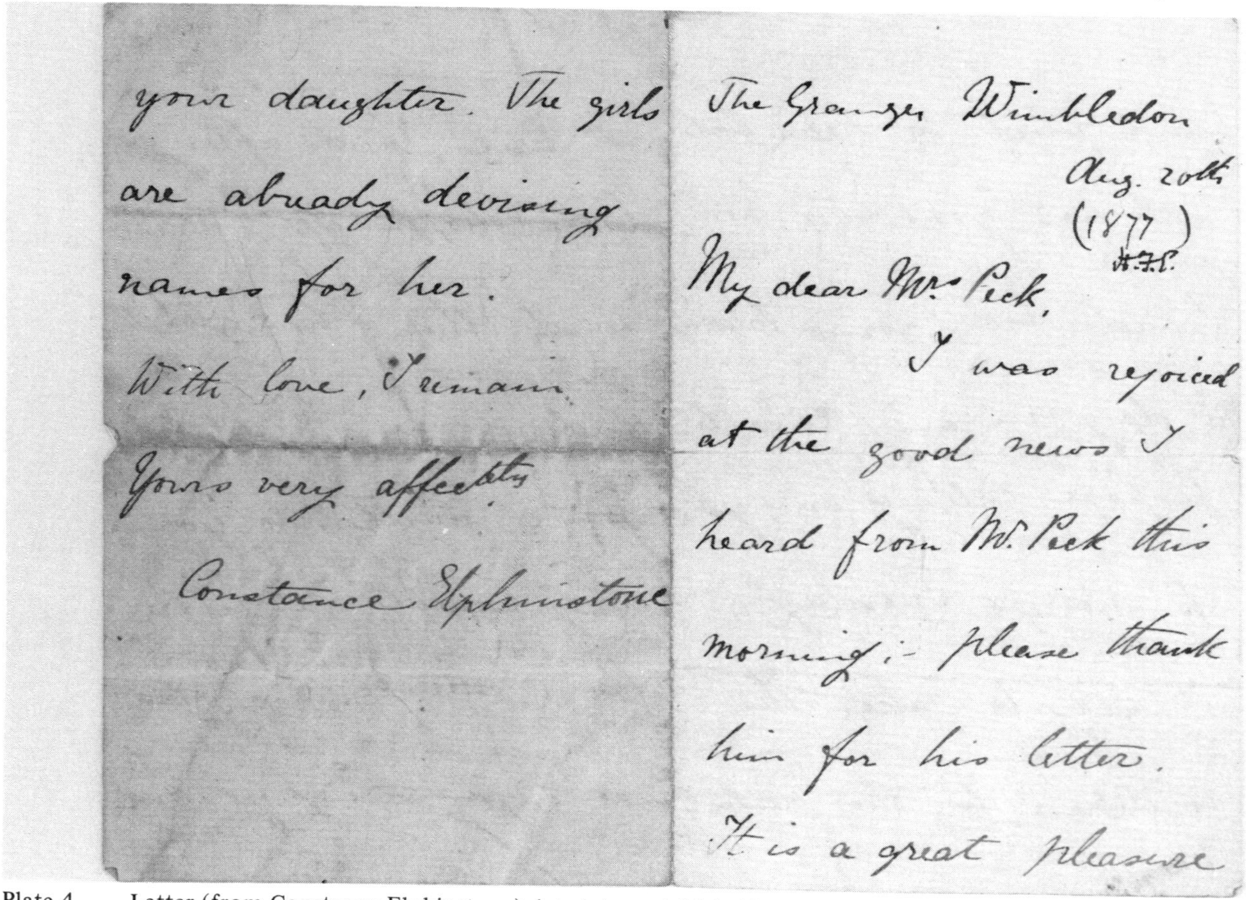
The Grange Wimbledon
Aug. 20th
(1877)
H.T.P.

My dear Mrs Peck,
I was rejoiced at the good news I heard from Mr Peck this morning :- please thank him for his letter.
It is a great pleasure

your daughter. The girls are already devising names for her.
With love, I remain
Yours very affectly
Constance Elphinstone

Plate 4 Letter (from Constance Elphinstone) dated August 20th 1877, headed 'The Grange'. (Front & Back)

and relief to hear that all has gone on well. I had been going to write to-day in any case to propose calling on you to-morrow, Tuesday. I have to take the children to the dentist at there, and after a little shopping, I shall and them home together, and come to pay you a visit, so you may expect me before five, I think, I shall so enjoy seeing you and

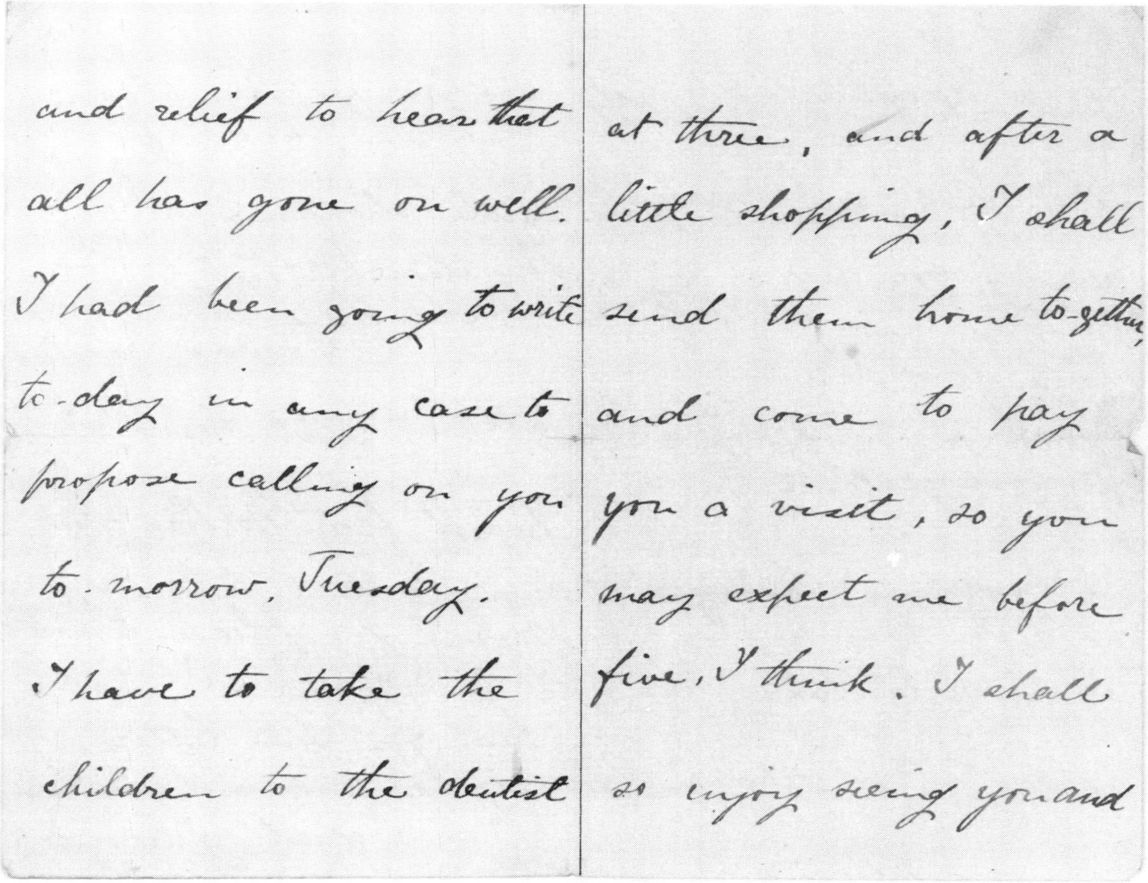

Plate 4A   Letter (from Constance Elphinstone) dated August 20th 1877, headed 'The Grange'. (Middle section)

Plate 5   The Auction Mart, St Bartholomew's Lane, (Throgmorton Street)   Engraving by W. Watkins   c. 1844

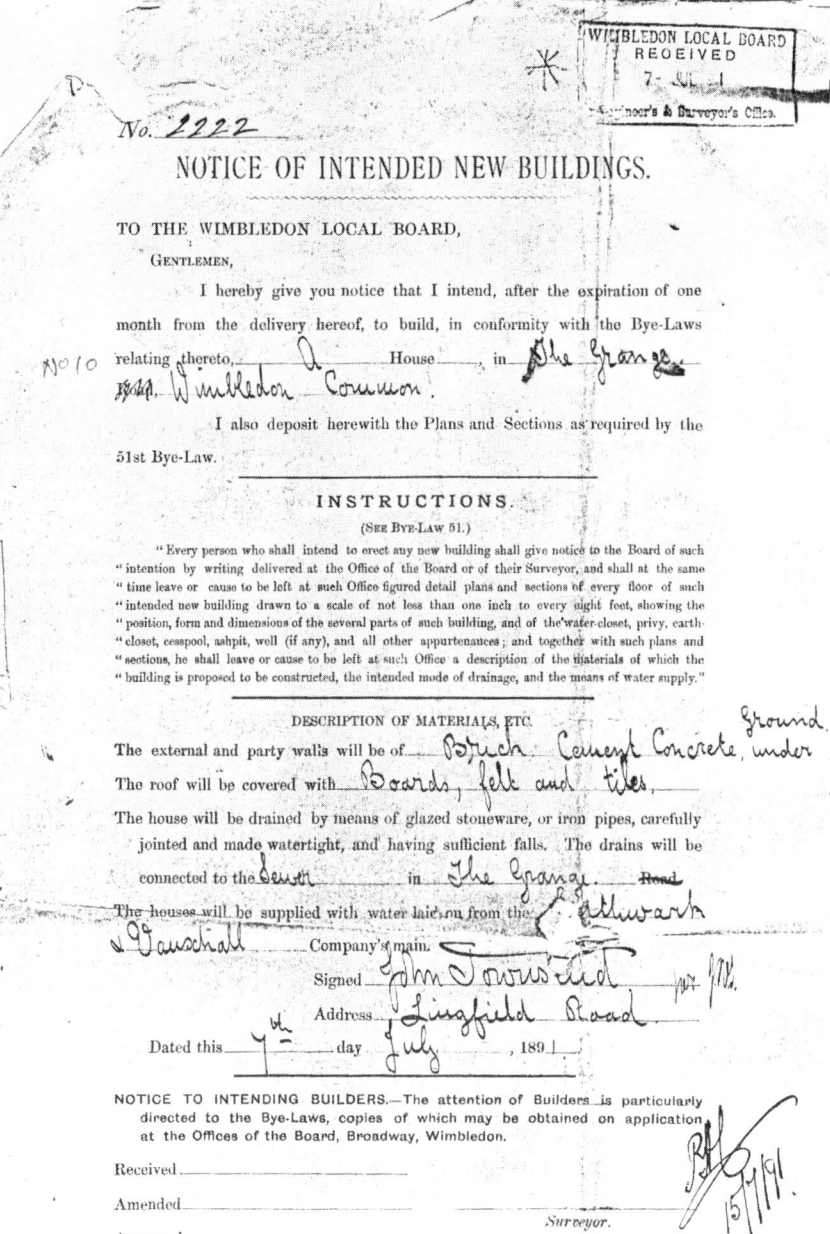

No. *2222*

NOTICE OF INTENDED NEW BUILDINGS.

TO THE WIMBLEDON LOCAL BOARD,

GENTLEMEN,

I hereby give you notice that I intend, after the expiration of one month from the delivery hereof, to build, in conformity with the Bye-Laws relating thereto, *a* House *in The Grange* *Wimbledon Common.*

I also deposit herewith the Plans and Sections as required by the 51st Bye-Law.

INSTRUCTIONS.

(SEE BYE-LAW 51.)

" Every person who shall intend to erect any new building shall give notice to the Board of such " intention by writing delivered at the Office of the Board or of their Surveyor, and shall at the same " time leave or cause to be left at such Office figured detail plans and sections of every floor of such " intended new building drawn to a scale of not less than one inch to every eight feet, showing the " position, form and dimensions of the several parts of such building, and of the water-closet, privy, earth- " closet, cesspool, ashpit, well (if any), and all other appurtenances ; and together with such plans and " sections, he shall leave or cause to be left at such Office a description of the materials of which the " building is proposed to be constructed, the intended mode of drainage, and the means of water supply."

DESCRIPTION OF MATERIALS, ETC.

The external and party walls will be of *Brick Cement Concrete, under Ground.*

The roof will be covered with *Boards, felt and tiles,*

The house will be drained by means of glazed stoneware, or iron pipes, carefully jointed and made watertight, and having sufficient falls. The drains will be connected to the *Sewer* in *The Grange* ~~Road~~

The houses will be supplied with water laid on from the *Southwark & Vauxhall* Company's main.

Signed *John Townsend* per *M.*

Address *Lingfield Road*

Dated this *7th* day *July* , 189 *1*

NOTICE TO INTENDING BUILDERS.—The attention of Builders is particularly directed to the Bye-Laws, copies of which may be obtained on application at the Offices of the Board, Broadway, Wimbledon.

Received

Amended

Approved

Surveyor.

21 (...)

Plate 6

Notice dated July 7th 1891 to Wimbledon Local Board of Intended New Buildings

89

Plate 7   'Grangemuir' (1889) by Weatherall & Green.
                 Back of house & garden prior to conversion.

90

Plate 8   No. 1 The Grange, Wimbledon (1889) by Aston Webb

Plate 9

No. 2 The Grange, Wimbledon (1889) by Edward J. May

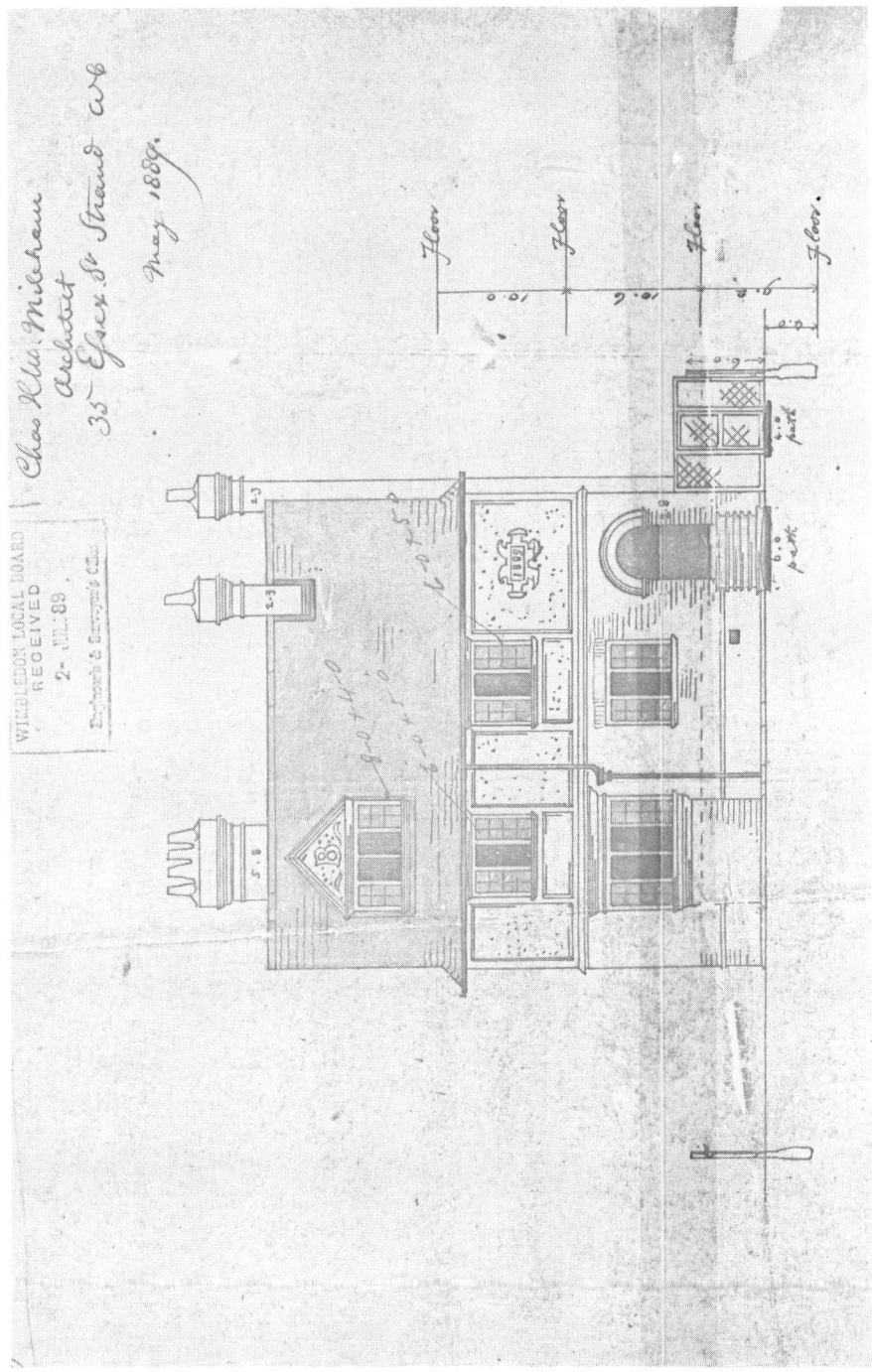

Plate 13   No. 23 The Grange, Wimbledon (1889) by Charles Mileham.   Front (north east) Elevation – original plan.

93

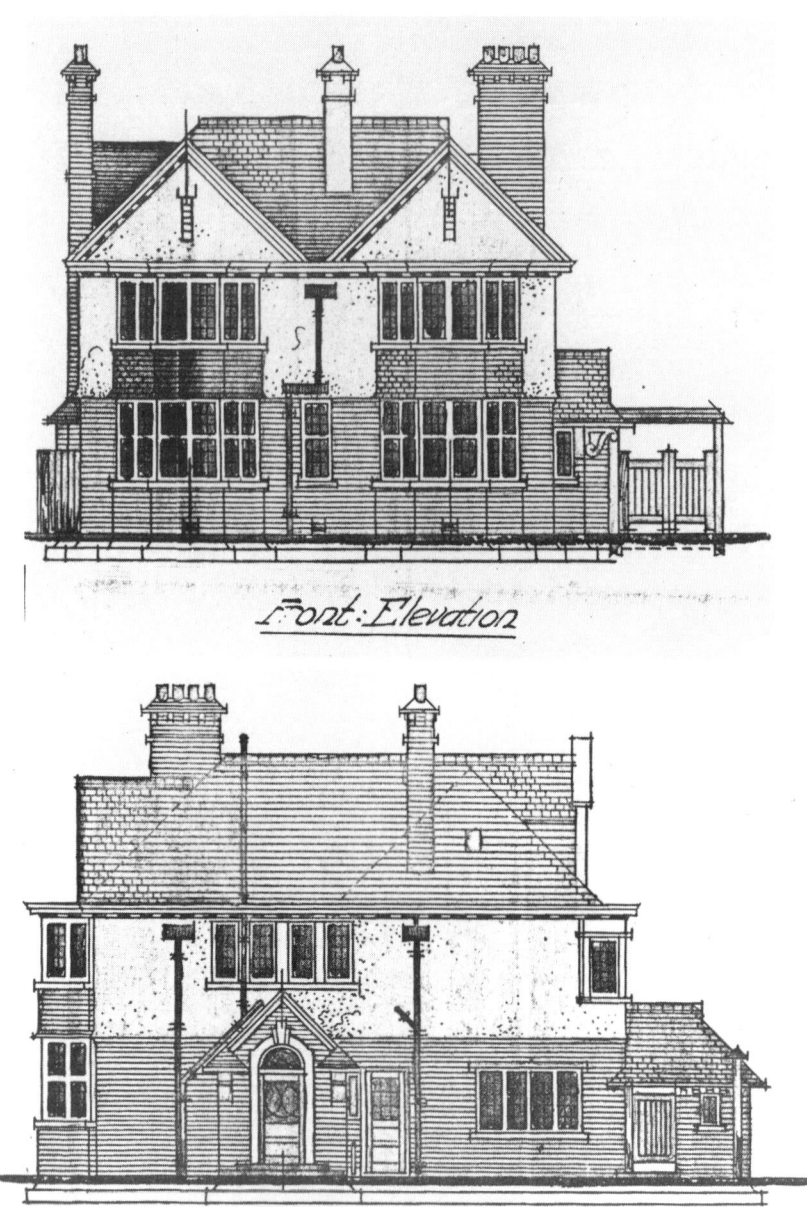

Front : Elevation

Side : Elevation

Plate 11   No. 4 The Grange, Wimbledon (1908) by G. Hubbard & A. Moore.
Front & side Elevations – original plans

Plate 12   No. 6 The Grange, Wimbledon (1889) by Henry Harmer.
             Front showing junction with No. 5

95

Plate 13

No. 7 The Grange, Wimbledon (1889) by Ernest Newton.

96

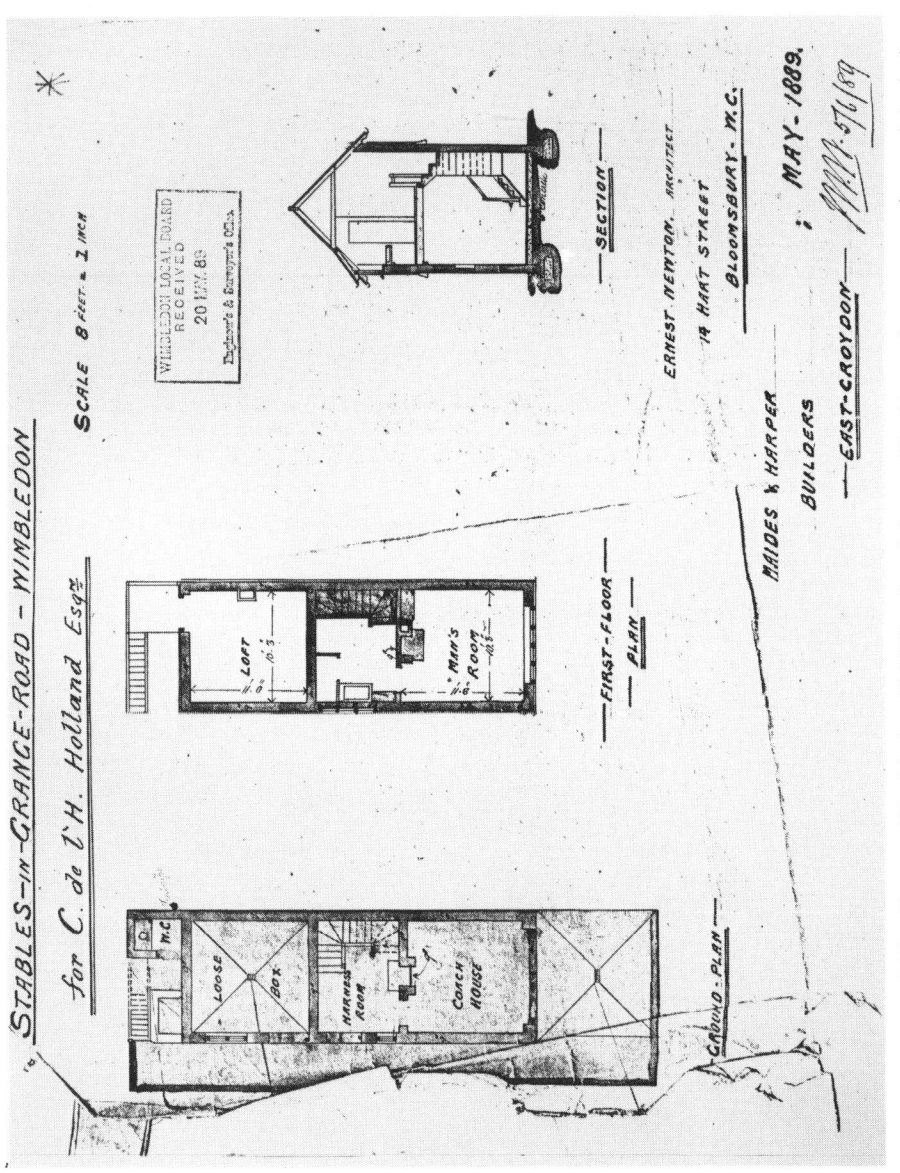

Plate 14   No. 7 The Grange, Wimbledon (1889)   Coach-house (Stables and rooms over) — original plans

97

Plate 15   Authors outside converted Coach-house, 7, The Grange, Wimbledon. (1984).

Plate 16

No. 8 The Grange, Wimbledon (1889) by John Townsend
Front of house with 'Whyteleafe' on gate & No. 7's coach-house in background

Front Elevation

Side Elevation

Plate 17   No. 9 The Grange, Wimbledon (1889) by John Townsend
            Front and side Elevations – original plans.

100

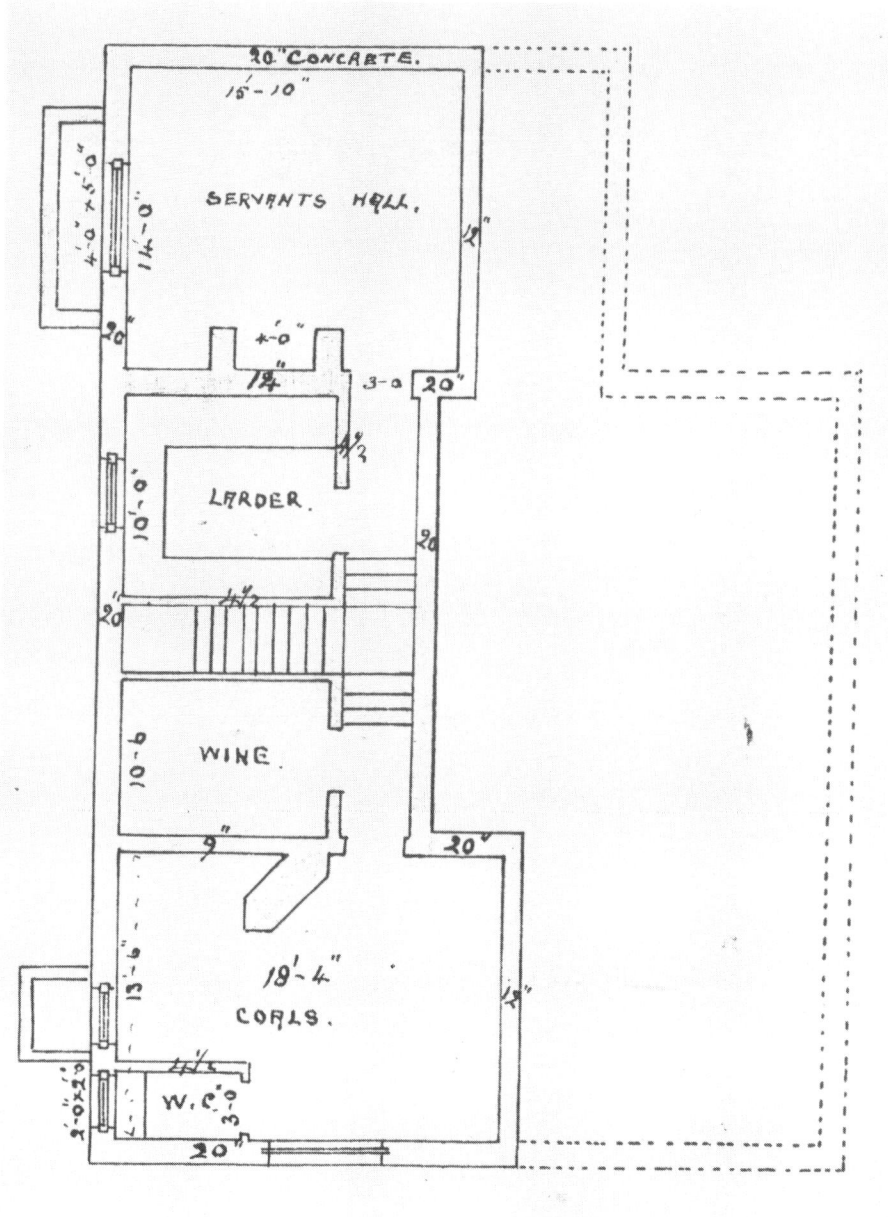

20" CONCRETE.

15'-10"

SERVANTS HALL.

14'-0"

4'-0" x 5'-0"

2'-0"

4'-0"

1'4"

3-0   20"

LARDER.

10'-0"

4'-2"

20"

20"

1'4½"

WINE.

10'-6"

9"

20"

13'-6"

18'-4"

COALS.

1'4½"

W.C.   3'-0"

2'-0" x 2'-0"

20"

CELLARAGE   PLAN.

Plate 18   No. 10 The Grange, Wimbledon (1891) by John Townsend
                Original cellar plan

101

Plate 19
'Grange Lodge', The Grange, Wimbledon (1890) by J. Wimperis & W. Arber now demolished. South front Elevation — original plan

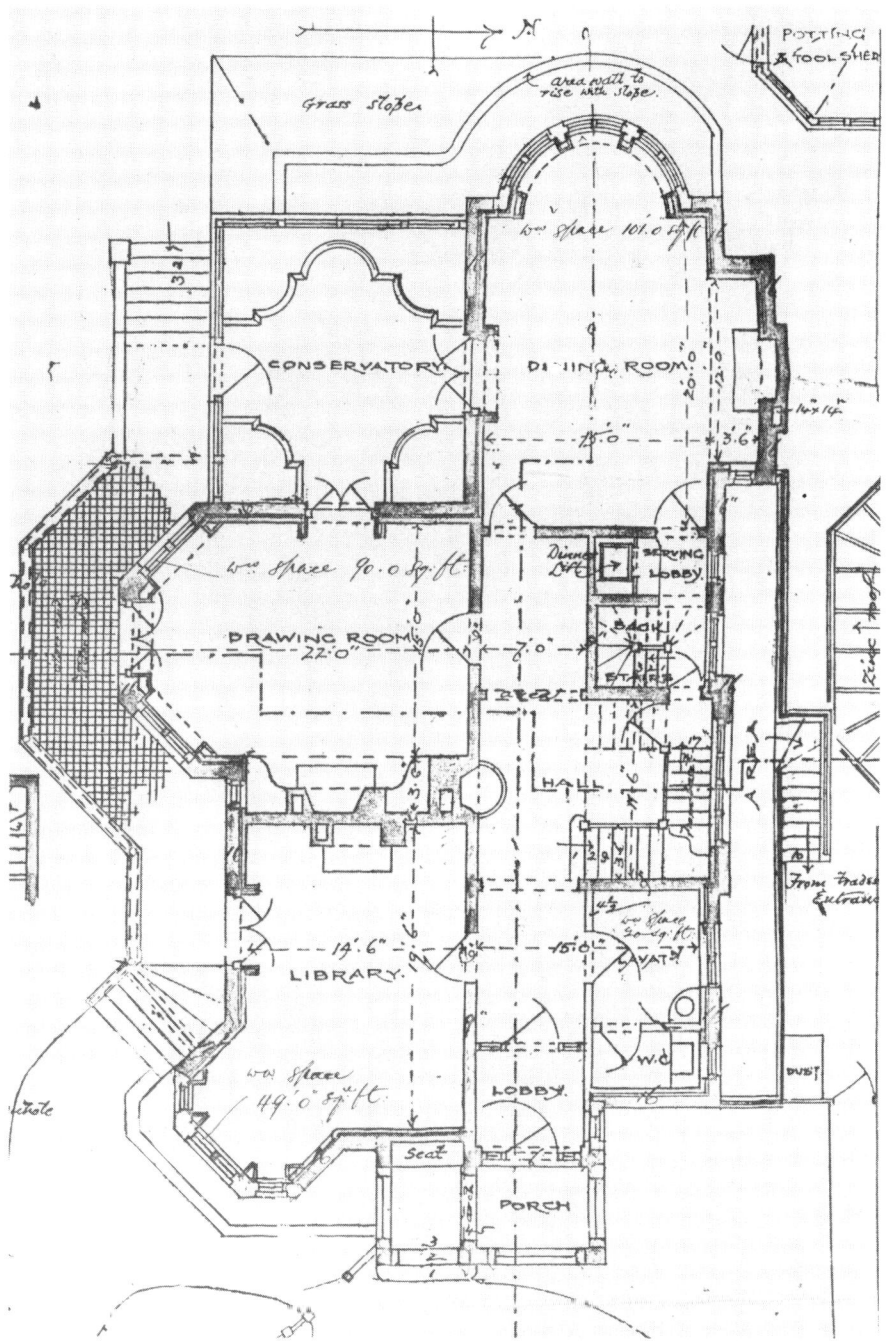

Plate 20   'Grange Lodge'   Ground Floor original plan

Plate 21   No. 15 The Grange, Wimbledon (1889) by Richard Creed   Side of house c. 1950

Plate 22   No. 18 The Grange, Wimbledon (1893) by Arthur Cawston

Appendix I

First Schedule to an Indenture of Conveyance dated 18th December 1888.

'Building lines for the Grange Estate. The building line (in respect of Lots 74—114 inclusive) is set back Twenty feet to the Grange.

The Grange Estate. No building shall be erected (on Lots 74—114 inclusive) of less value than Eight hundred pounds respectively. The value of a building on these estates is the amount of its net first cost in materials and labour of construction only estimated at the lowest current prices.

Character of buildings. No building except private residences and their outbuildings shall be erected on any of the lots and no trade or manufacture shall be carried out on nor any operative machinery fixed or placed on any lot. No hut shed caravan house on wheels or other chattel adapted or intended for use as a dwelling or sleeping apartment shall be erected made placed or used or to be allowed to remain on any Lot and the Vendor or the Owner or the Owners of any part of the said lot may remove and dispose of any such erection or other thing and for that purpose may break fences and forcibly enter any land upon which a breach of stipulation shall occur and shall not be responsible for the safe keeping of anything so removed or for the loss thereof or any damage thereto.

Maintenance of Roads Paths and Sewers. The purchaser of each or any lot shall until the roads and sewers on the estate have been adopted by the Local Authorities contribute his fair proportion towards maintaining and repairing the same the amount of such contribution to be settled by the Vendors Surveyors.

No road or cartway shall be made on any lot.'

These covenants applied to all the lots of land other than the Southside lots which had frontages on to Wimbledon Common. These more desirable sites had the same covenants except that no building was to be erected 'of less value than One thousand five hundred pounds'.

However by the time the land for No. 18 was sold by Henry Harmer to Arthur Cawston to build his house in 1892 i.e some 4 years later, the covenant states that the house was to be not less than £1000 in value. No doubt this was the £800 figure 'index linked'.

Information Service of the Royal Institution of Chartered Surveyors. No information is available on building costs before 1896, but their experts have calculated that building costs of £800 and £1500 in 1888 would approximate to £67,000 and £125,000 in 1983.

Without a doubt, in practice, most if not all the houses were built to a higher standard, and therefore at higher cost than the minimum covenant figures of £800 and £1500.

The £800 figure related to the originally proposed 50 feet frontage lots, and for some semi-detached housing.

Basten, Harmer's foreman-carpenter

Apart from his business in The Grange, the only thing we know about Harmer's firm/ employees comes from the sorry story related at Surrey Quarter Sessions in July, 1890. It conveys the flavour of the social sub-culture of the time.

A man named George Basten, and his second wife, were tried on a charge of cruelty and starvation of Basten's son by his first wife, Ernest, aged 12. Basten had become foreman carpenter to Henry Harmer. Ernest, though aged 12, had been found by the Society for the prevention of cruelty to children to weigh only 38lbs. The other children in the family were in good condition. Basten had been working for Harmer since March 1887, for an average wage of £2.00 per week. Basten's second wife said she had had four children since her marriage, two living, one of 5 and the other of 2 years old. Basten had not come home to dinner for the last two years. During the time he had been out of work, being absent on account of illness from July to December (?1889), no money was coming in but what friends sent; and it had made a difference to her ability to provide for the children. There was enough food for all; but she deposed that Ernest was of dirty habits. George Basten, the boy's father, testified that his first wife had died seven years ago, and he had married again in 1881. The money was too great for him to send the boy to the (St. Marylebone) Industrial School. Since November (?1889) he had had to pay off debts of £50 that had accrued during his long illness. After a 15 minutes recess the jury returned a verdict of guilty on both George and Mrs. Basten. The judge imposed a sentence of 6 months with hard labour on both. The male prisoner appeared exceedingly surprised at the sentence imposed. In the following week, the Wandsworth Police Court granted custody of Ernest to the Secretary of the Society for the Prevention of Cruelty to Children.

Appendix III

Architects of Houses in The Grange, Wimbledon.

Arthur Cawston (1857—1894)
A short life of 37 years, which ended in tragic circumstances at his office in 13 Queen Anne's Gate, did not enable him to reach the higher echelons in the Royal Institute of British Architects (R.I.B.A.), and knowledge about his activities is somewhat limited. However, amongst his works concurrent with No. 18 which he designed for himself and his family, were a market in Fisher Street, Carlisle; St. Lukes Church, Bromley Common; and the Ascension Church and Vicarage, Malwood Road, Balham Hill. He was also the author of 'A Comprehensive Scheme for London Street Improvements'. He left £11,853.

Richard Creed F.R.I.B.A. (1846—1914)
The architect of Nos. 17 and 15 seems to have had personal connections with the families at these houses. He was mainly a domestic architect, as his works from 1873—1882 cited on his candidature statement of December 1881 for admission to Fellowship of the R.I.B.A. show. The houses mentioned were mainly in Sussex and Surrey. Of interest to Wimbledonians, he designed a fishing box on the River Wandle. His proposer stated that his work'. . . bears the impress of an artisitic mind and careful design.' He died at his last home at Little Bardfield Hall, Essex, leaving £14,041.

George Hubbard F.S.A. (1859—1936) and *Albert W. Moore F.R.I.B.A.* (1876—1965)
These architects designed No. 4 in 1908 before their partnership was dissolved. Hubbard then took his son Philip into his firm. Hubbard and Moore also made the plans for later houses in Wimbledon, for example the Old Pound House and other houses on Parkside, Parkside Gardens and Peek Crescent. Hubbard was a combination of antiquary and artist. Amongst his own work were the Ironmongers Almshouses at Mottingham, a charming house (Stuart House) at Cambridge. Probate was granted to his architect son Philip — £33,217. Albert W. Moore's best-known later work was the Oxo Warehouse. He died at the age of 91 in his White Cottage at Walton-on-Thames, leaving £31,383.

Edward John May F.R.I.B.A. (1853—1941)
The architect of Nos. 2, 3, and 24 was chiefly a domestic architect, who also designed 4 Southside, Wimbledon (1900) now much altered, as well as other houses in Surrey and in almost every county in England. He became a Fellow in 1887. He was a pupil of Decimus Burton (a founder member of the R.I.B.A. in 1834), whose biography he later wrote. On completion of his articles, May went to work at Norman Shaw's office. Through Shaw, he became architect to the newly formed Bedford Park Estate, and lived in Queen Anne's Grove there before coming to Wimbledon, to live at No. 2, which he called 'Lyneham'. He did not enter competitions for public work, although he did hold the post of Consulting Architect to the Church of England Waifs and Strays Society. He was one of the best known men of the day, but he was a modest man. An obituary says of him, 'For him architecture to the end remained just an absorbing craft, which, with his family and home, his garden and his deep religion, filled a most joyous life to overflowing'. He died in March 1941 at his home in Chislehurst, Kent which he had also called 'Lyneham', leaving £4,023.

Charles Henry Money Mileham (1837–1917)
The architect of No. 23 was working from 35 Essex Street, Strand in the 1880s to 1890s at least. With some difficulty we have discovered something of this unassuming man who never asserted the position to which his work entitled him. He was largely engaged in domestic architecture and the design of small public buildings, in particular schools and churches. At the time when he designed No. 23, he was carrying out his best and most characteristic work at St. Albans, Holborn, both the St. Albans Schools and St. Alban-the-Martyr Church, Holborn. He also painted charming water colours. He died in December 1917 when his home was near Hampstead Heath, leaving the very modest sum of £2,225.

Ernest Newton, C.B.E., R.A., F.R.I.B.A. (1856–1922)
The architect of No. 7 was articled to Norman Shaw in 1873, and set up in his own practice in 1879. He was a founder member of the Art Workers' Guild, and an early member of the Arts and Crafts Society. He held the post of President of the R.I.B.A. from 1914–1918. Mainly a domestic architect, he designed many private houses, mostly in the Home Counties. Like his contemporary fellow architect, E.J. May, he had Dutch connections, having married Antoinette, daughter of a merchant of Rotterdam. He died at his house in Maida Vale, with the surprisingly small effects of £11,313, unlike Aston Webb (q.v.)

Sir Aston Webb K.C.V.O., C.B., R.A., F.R.I.B.A. (1849–1930)
This architect of No. 1 set up practice in London in 1873. He gained many honours, and was President of the Architectural Association in 1884, President of the R.I.B.A. from 1902–4, being knighted in the latter year, and President of the Royal Academy in 1919–24. He is not known principally as a domestic architect, his main works being public buildings, including the Birmingham Law Courts (1887–91), the Victoria and Albert Museum (1891) (more or less contemporary with No. 1), Birmingham University (1900–09) with E. Ingress Bell, and the refacing of Buckingham Palace (1913). He died at his house in Hanover Terrace, Ladbroke Square, Notting Hill in August 1930. Probate was given to his architect son, Maurice Everett Webb, with effects of £98,380.

John Thomas Wimperis F.R.I.B.A. (1831–1904) and
William Henry Arber F.R.I.B.A. (1849–1904)
The architects of the original 'Grange Lodge' in 1890 were still in partnership, but it was dissolved in 1897. Wimperis had been elected a Fellow in 1877. Arber had been articled to Wimperis from 1866, then becoming his assistant, and subsequently his partner in 1889, just before this house was designed. Wimperis was the more important of the two, and had planned an enormous number of buildings in inner London, many of them mansions rather than villas, in the Grosvenor Square/Berkeley Square areas for example. Unlike any of the other architects of houses in The Grange, Wimperis made plans for London clubs, hotels and music halls. He died at Half Moon Street, Piccadilly, leaving £51,430. Arber was elected a Fellow in 1893, being proposed by Wimperis. Obviously he was associated with many of the works of his senior partner, including the Mayfair houses and flats, and the Grafton Galleries. Wimperis and Arber died within a few months of each other.

Appendix IV

The Murray Road Story

The Murray Road story had its origins in the story of 'Wimbledon Lodge' (Murray House) (1797–1904). Together with its grounds, the Murray House Estate stretched from Wimbledon Common Southside across the Ridgway as far south as the contour ridge itself, the particular piece from the estate boundary east-west along the ridge becoming St. John's Road. Murray House must have been thought of in its heyday as *like* 'The Grange' house, but *superior* to it.

We need not go into the history of Murray House, designed by the architect Aaron Henry Hurst (1762–1799). The long years of the Murray family occupancy of the house, and indeed the house itself, came to an end in 1904 with the death of Miss Gertrude Murray, the daughter of General Sir Henry Murray and granddaughter of Gerard de Visme who had it built.

It was at Miss Murray's death that the British Land Company (B.L.C.) came on the scene. The B.L.C. was born in the 1860s, a brainchild of Wright and Cobden. After the Reform Act of 1832, land tenure of a certain acreage was a pre-requisite for the acquisition of the privilege of the parliamentary suffrage. 'Buying Votes' was prohibited by the first Reform Act. *Creating* votes was *not.*

Much of North Wimbledon had already been developed between 1888 and 1904. First, The Grange estate; then the Wimbledon House estate. Third, the Belvedere estate on the east side of Wimbledon High Street to the north end of Wimbledon Hill Road. This pattern of rapid, successive suburban development was replicated elsewhere, while the right to vote hardly changed. *Property* as well as *male sex qualifications* remained requirements for the parliamentary suffrage. To people whose political stance was against that of the Conservative-Unionists, just as much as those who favoured that cause, the result in Wimbledon, at the time of the parliamentary election landslide in 1906, must have been interpreted as indicating that North Wimbledon was well on the way to becoming pretty solidly conservative in terms of votes.

The B.L.C., through its acquisition and layout of the Murray House estate, made a belated effort to leaven the conservative lump. Rights to vote were slowly democratised by successive reform Acts during the fifty most active years of operation of the B.L.C. from its foundation until 1919. But the very process of widening of the suffrage base meant that when the time came to develop the Murray Road estate, the B.L.C. was satisfied with the creation of landholdings generally *just a bit smaller* than those of The Grange, which, as we have seen, were acutely responsive to middle class market demand.

The way the Murray Road development worked out, as seems so often to be the case, began with one model and pattern; but a section of it displays clear signs of early compromises being made with first principles in the light of prevailing market forces. Thus, at the auction of lots for the Murray Road development in 1906, the lots on the *west* side of Murray Road (i.e. properties whose gardens would back onto those of properties on the *east* side of Lauriston Road), and lots on the *east* side of Murray Road, from the back of 'Wolstan', No. 19, The Grange, southwards to the Ridgway, both had *50* feet frontages. But the Murray Road lots northwards towards Southside from a point drawn east to No. 7, The Grange, and on the exact parallel west from there across Murray Road, were both more *varied*, and all with a *longer* frontage; and seem to have corresponded roughly to the length of frontages of the houses on the same parallels in The Grange. Doubtless some purchasers of lots at the Murray Road auction of 1906, and subsequently, bought more than a single 50 feet frontage lot. However, those, just at that point further south from Wimbledon Common Southside, must have confined their purchase to a 50 feet frontage only.

The most important documentation of the Murray House estate development is fortunately deposited in the collection of the Wimbledon Society in its Museum of local history.

The varying strengths of the several forces at work in the development, auctions, and subsequent sales, as between The Grange and Murray Road, accounted for the differences, subtle as these may nowadays be felt to be, between the two roads. Doubtless, analysis of the development of say, Lingfield Road, which one of us has already examined, Lauriston Road, Clifton Road, and roads from the Ridgway south to the escarpment, would yield similarly rewarding material for comparative study.

Appendix V

The 'Cygnets' School at No. 22

The oral evidence (November 1983) of Flavia, widow of Humphrey Nunes, who had grown up in No. 22 The Grange in the 1930s, was that when their daughter was five years old, in 1950, they set up a home-school for their children, and those of like minded parents, in their dining-room. It figured as a Parents' National Educational Union (P.N.E.U.)* school in a list of P.N.E.U. schools, being registered as one of four such in London, catering for Boys and Girls, Preparatory (5 years) and Form 1 (6—8 years). That agrees with our aural recollection of it, our home, No. 7 being almost opposite No. 22. We also remember that at some point, one of the Nunes parents called at No. 7 to check that residents would make no objection to the use of residential premises as a home-school. This must have been either when the dining room of No. 22 was put to such use; or when they extended, later, into the use of the semi-basement of No. 6, exactly opposite to No. 22. It continued until their departure to Kensington in 1962. The P.N.E.U. list also shows the school as having a Charlotte Mason Teacher on the staff. It was called the 'Cygnets'. In a letter of March 1981 Flavia Nunes recalled 'Most of the time (the 'Cygnets' was) under the unique Miss Audrey Smith (who) still hears from many ex-pupils. They really have been amazingly successful — partly Miss Smith but also because Rokeby sent us a lot of very bright children to get ready for them.' Rokeby was then at the foot of The Downs, Wimbledon, a stone's throw from Worple Road, a preparatory school for boys (7 – 13 years). The Downs also houses the Ursuline Convent school for girls.

* Now called the World-wide Education Service of the P.N.E.U.

112

Appendix VI

The Clergy Sons of No. 7

James Burnes Holland (1883–1956) read modern history at University College, Oxford, got a third in 1905, then went to Ely Theological College in 1907. From 1908–1913 he worked, in what was then the fashionable church of St. Saviour's, Pimlico; then in an assistant priest's post in another St. Saviour's, Hoxton, one of the churches built by Robert Brett in the 1860s under the Haggerston Church scheme, that had taken its inspiration from the Oxford Movement. The Hoxton parish was as far unlike North Wimbledon as could be found. Christian settlements were then common in the East End, staffed with bachelors, worker priests before that term became normal. James stayed a bachelor. St. Saviour's, Hoxton, was not a settlement *per se*. The church itself was damaged in the second World War and demolished after 1960; the clergy house was attached. James must have lived in that. In those days, Hoxton and Shoreditch were like a sardine tin of terraced houses interspersed with workshops. In 1861, the official guide recorded that 'the population of Shoreditch reached the fantastic total of 129,000 people in an area of only 640 acres'. James officiated in autumn 1913 at the marriage of two waitresses, the first to a salesman, the second to a surgical instrument maker. A month after his elder brother's death, he was the priest at the wedding of a private in the Dorset Regiment. Till June, 1916, he conducted between one and four marriage ceremonies per month. Then he became a temporary chaplain to the forces (T.C.F.) until 1919; returning thence to Hoxton; continuing with his former type of work till at least October 1919 and almost certainly until after his father's probate was settled in 1923. In the following year James was converted to Roman Catholicism. In 1925 he entered Brompton Oratory as a priest, remaining there until he had to enter a nursing home for what was to prove a long mental illness. He died at 54, Marine Parade, Brighton, in January 1956, possessed of effects of £23,736, aged 72.

The elder Sheldon son, the Reverend Frederick Howard, took his B.A. in 1908, at Trinity College Cambridge. (His father had taken his in 1884 at Queen's). Thence he went to Ridley Hall, Cambridge, for his theological course. After various curate or vicar posts in Marylebone, Richmond, Lambeth and Mitcham he was appointed in 1929 District Secretary, British Foreign and Bible Society, for South Metropolitan Kent and Sussex; from 1933 to 1941 was Vicar of St. John the Evangelist, Blackheath; then Rector of Maresfield, near Reigate and finally Vicar of Reigate from 1947.

The younger Sheldon son, the Reverend Leonard Gordon Melville, was similarly a Cambridge man. Leonard took his B.A. at Trinity College, a third in Part 1 of his History tripos, a second in Part 2, in 1914. He went straight on to theological college, Ridley Hall, as had done his elder brother; qualified thence in 1915; had an easier passage thereafter into vicarages and the T.C.F. (1917 to 1920), doubtless because he could draw on his relatives' experience and on account of the manpower-shortage of the times at which he was coming on to the labour market. He was curate at Christ Church, Croydon, from 1915 to 1920; thereafter, with his brother from 1920 to

1923, at the time the family bought No. 7, The Grange, Vicar of Christ Church, Mitcham.   Then for six years until 1929, vicar of Emmanuel, Northwood, Derby. Thence, Rector of Cheltenham until 1936.   Thereafter Vicar of Crowborough, in the diocese of Chichester.   This helps to account for the place of death of his father in June, 1942.   Leonard had clearly learned how to butter parsnips in the inter-war Anglican scene.   He had a patron, according to the 1941 Crockford's Clerical Directory, to wit, the Marquis of Abergavenny; so had his line firmly out into the old regime; yet was also well in with the coming system.   For of his total income (gross), in 1941, of £522, or £477 plus house, in a parish with a population of just under 5,000, he drew £303 from the Ecclesiasitcal Commission, got £19 in fees; another £200 from two well-heeled sources.   His address in 1941 was the Vicarage, Crowborough, Sussex.

1) Authors' Note

The Grange, Wimbledon, a centenary portrait is *not* an academic thesis.   We lack space to cite the source of each of the facts we have adduced, and of every quotation used. Everything, however, is as authentic as if it had been a university thesis.   If we were asked, we could identify the reference on which we have drawn at any point in this study.   Our sources concern the relevant times and places (both The Grange itself, and related spots whose historical and geographical situation appeared sufficiently comparable to justify reference).   They range from the general, e.g. Paul Thompson's *The Edwardians'*, to the highly specific and particular, e.g. Ernest Newton's architectural drawings for the construction in 1889 of No. 7, The Grange.

We have tried, in the following instancing, to present a selective, but sufficiently complete, citation of both general and particularly useful specific sources.   The reader is also referred to our prefatory acknowledgements, appendices, and occasional footnotes.

2) Published Materials

(a) *Books,* etc.

Bartlett, William A., *History and antiquities of Wimbledon*, 1865, republished, S.R. Publishers Ltd., 1971.

Copeland, Henry v.d.B.(ed) *Wimbledon & Merton Annual*, 1903, 04, 05, 10, Edwin Trim & Co. etc.

Dymond, David, *Writing local history*, Bedford Square Press, 1981

Dyos, H.J., *Victorian suburb*, Leicester University Press, 1961

Dyos, H.J. & Wolff, M. (eds), *The Victorian City, images & realities*, R.K.P., 1973

Fawcett, Patrick, *Memories of a Wimbledon childhood*, John Evelyn Society, 1981

Glass, Ruth, (ed), *London, aspects of change*, Centre for urban studies, McGibbon & Kee, 1964

'M.G.', *Viewpoints in & around Wimbledon*, The Hill Bookshop, 1925

Graves, Robert, *Goodbye to all that*, Cape, 1929, Cassell, 1957, Penguin Books, 1975

Jenkins, Simon, *Landlords to London*, Constable, 1975

Lewis, Roy, & Maude, Angus, *The English middle classes*, Penguin Books, 1953

Masterman, C.F.G., *The condition of England*, Methuen, 1909 & 1911

Milward, Richard, *Foreword* to Bartlett's *History, supra*, 1971

Norman, Frank, *Whitehall to West Indies*, Bodley Head, 1952

Oliver, P., Davis, I., & Bentley, I., *Dunroamin*, Barrie & Jenkins, 1981

Plastow, Norman, *Safe as houses; Wimbledon, 1939–1945*, John Evelyn Society 1972

Ravensdale, J., *History on your doorstep*, B.B.C., Jenkins, 1982

Simpson, M.A., & Lloyd, T.H., (eds), *Middle class housing in Britain*, David & Charles, 1977

Sitwell, Osbert, *Before the bombardment*, Penguin Books, 1938

Thompson, F.M.L. (ed.), *The rise of suburbia*, Leicester University Press, 1982

Thompson, Paul, *The Edwardians*, Weidenfeld & Nicolson, 1975

Veblen, Thorstein, *The theory of the leisure class*, first pub., 1899, repub., 1973, Houghton Mifflin Co., Boston, with an intro. by J.K. Galbraith

Young, Michael, & Willmott, Peter, *The symmetrical family*, R.K.P., 1973 & Penguin Books, 1975

(b) *Dictionaries, directories, lists*
(from Wimbledon Public Reference Library, Surrey County Record Office, and Guildhall Library, except where otherwise indicated)

Army Lists

Bankers Almanac

Biographical Dictionary of British Architects, 1600–1840, Murray, 1978

Burke's Peerage & Baronetcy

Cherry, Bridget, & Pevsner, Nikolaus & Ian Nairn, *The Buildings of England, London 2 – South*, Penguin Books, 1983

Crockford's Clerical Directories

Dictionary of National Biography

Dixon, Roger, and Muthesius, Stefan, *Victorian Architecture*, Thames & Hudson, 1978

John Evelyn Society, Annual reports

Kelly's Directories

Law Lists

Parish Registers, Wimbledon, County of Surrey

Post Office Directories

Trim's Directories

Ware, Dora, *Short dictionary of British architects*, G. Allen & Unwin, 1967

Who was who

(c) *Government & local government publications & records*

H.M.S.O., Registrar General, Censuses of population, 1851 to 1881

H.M.S.O., Electoral registers, 1888 to present

H.M.S.O., Officers died in the Great War

H.M.S.O., Ordnance Survey, *Maps, 1865 to present*

H.M.S.O., *Registers of births, deaths & marriages*

H.M.S.O., Registrar General, *Wills*

Wimbledon Borough Council, *Wimbledon Charter Jubilee, 1905–1955*, Malcolm Page Ltd.

Wimbledon Local Board, *Annual reports, minutes, rate-books*

3) Unpublished Sources

(a) *Architects' drawings & surveyors' plans etc.*

Richard Roberts, *report and plan for the development of The Grange estate.* 24th September, 1886

Architects (various) & surveyors (various):– see text

Drawings for the houses constructed in The Grange, 1889 to 1908:– see text and plates

Hampton & Sons, Estate agents' books

(b) *Manuscripts, theses, etc.*

Cooke, Penelope Warner, *The history of a country seat and its development; study of part of a London suburb*; mimeo, 1973

Wimbledon Literary & Scientific Society, *Minutes*

(c) *Oral evidence*

From various sources referred to in the text

(d) *Property deeds etc.*

In respect of the various properties in The Grange and Murray Road, as referred to in the text.

4) Newspapers, journals, periodicals etc.

The Architect & Building News

The Builder

Journal of the Royal Institute of British Architects.

Mid-Surrey Independent

The Times

Who's who in Architecture

Wimbledon News/Wimbledon Borough News (W.B.N.)

129

This index covers and is confined to: —

Grange Estate; Grange Preservation Association; Grange Road; 'The Grange' (18th century house); and The Grange (road) - general and houses.

For the following other Wimbledon roads - see under the relevant letter of the alphabet in the Main Index for Page references.

VG